One
of the
Many

*To - Rox
LeT us ConTiNue.
Michael J ScoTTs*

Michael J. Scott

PAGE PUBLISHING, INC.
Conneaut Lake, PA

First originally published by Page Publishing 2021

ISBN 978-1-6624-4913-0 (pbk)
ISBN 978-1-6624-4914-7 (digital)

Printed in the United States of America

ACKNOWLEDGMENTS

There are several that I wish to thank for their contributions that aided me in the process of retracing my steps back to humanity.

Mr. Richard Roma, now deceased, was my first initial contact to Page Publishing. It was he who responded to my inquiry and subsequently mentored me. With just a few hundred words typed, I had always received his inquiry of my health and that of my father, of whom I was the primary caretaker. What is most notable is that he always told me, "The story will write itself when all is properly in place," and he always reminded me at that time that I was called to take care of Dad. Richard, you were correct, and I thank you. Please tell Dad I miss him.

Matt and Madeline, friends, thank you for not only believing in me but also fighting the world for me. It was because of the both of you that I learned not to stay angry at injustice but to thrive despite it. I am learning to be kind and to be careful at the same time.

My youngest brother, Eric, though I was largely responsible for him missing the only surprise birthday party that our mother ever gave him, he forgave me. Now that this is complete, you can now read your second book. I don't know if it is better than *The Other Side of Midnight*, but it may be closer to home.

Mr. Mitchel, a.k.a. One L, I'm still alive. I am somewhere along the path.

Giant

INTRODUCTION

One of the Many may be considered an anthology of the travels of one man, one step at a time, into the descent of travails from humanity and his return, his ascent, back into the ranks of humanity. In each lifetime, there are moments that define the next. In some instances, these epiphanies or "Aha!" moments are times in which certain understandings are revealed. I have probably violated a writer's creed because I did not choose a targeted population to appeal to. Instead, I wrote these memoirs to leave a record to my family, the litany of my journeys of the good, the bad, and the ugly. Perhaps yield reason for how I am today and where I came from. Perhaps angels do walk among us, and perhaps God, in his infinite wisdom, assigns humans to fill in to help. Whatever it may be, I am certain that it is only through divine providence that I'm alive today. It is said that we are the sum total of all that we've experienced and all that we have truly learned. Again, this may be true—I can only speak for myself, a lowly man who forfeited promise and created an aftermath of destruction in my wake, trying to live. It was only in true submission that I found courage and resolve to reconstruct amending ways to aid and contribute to the living, where I have found a relative peace in an unpeaceful world. Come travel with me and attempt to fill the shoes of our characters and feel the air of their activities. It is not possible for me to remember all of it, but through my feeble attempts, maybe I can color the story of truth. These are few of the many events of my life; perhaps there are those who may identify with some of them. I have tried to tell it as it happened, and at times the language of these characters will be harsh. But no matter how they speak, they will always relay the truth. This, I believe, is just the first installment of relaying a thirty-year journey of one of the many.

————————————————————

CHAPTER 1

Awakening from the Dead

April 3, in the year of 2020, and another major life experience happened. Just one of many. Yet this occurrence would have a significant, immediate impact on a forthcoming cycle of events that would test all that I had ever learned and endured.

I stood in the early-morning hour of five o'clock and silently watched the strongest man I had ever met start to draw the last breaths of his magnificent life. An example of what it really meant to be a man, citizen, and husband, my father lay in a hospital bed in the room that he and my mother had shared for a great many years. I intently watched him, one hand placed gently on his head.

I whispered in hushed tones while stroking his hair, "It's okay, Pop. Go on. You've worked hard and raised two families, and we wanted for nothing. You have earned your rest. Mama, your mama, and all that went before you await your arrival. We will be all right. I know you're worried about me, but don't worry, you've given me the keys to live. Thank you for letting me come back home, and thank you for taking the time to teach me once again how to be a real man. I will be there for Melissa and Eric, I promise you. I will miss you, and I love you, but it would be selfish for me to ask you to stay."

Tears welled in my eyes and slowly slid down my cheeks. There were no prayers to be whispered as the dark angel quietly came into this realm. A deep breath and a long, slow exhale and my father was no more. With my hand still placed upon his head, I watched as a transformation of peace and the radiance of youthfulness replaced the toil of living on his face. Wiping my tears away with the back of my hand, I smiled even in my deeply grief-stricken state. With the evidence right before my own eyes, I'd seen life-to-death transition. The room, his bedroom, became the silence that only comes with the visitation of death, and the quality of the air became "suppressed," not with the lack of oxygen, but something other than this principal gas. One can only identify with this explanation if they have experienced death's presence up close and personal.

Seven years had passed since my return home, and for every moment, every hour, and every day since, I had been primary caregiver to this man, my father, my friend, my staunch supporter and example of how to be a man. And now he had quietly exited this thing called life.

I stood silently and witnessed on his face the peace that only death can bring, saw the tension of pain and struggle ease in moments of surrender. I intently watched as old age succumbed to the inner youth and lines of age smoothed out into delicate folds of peace, and through trickling tears I felt the transition from the living to the dead. Pop was ninety-six years old, and I placed my hand upon his head and knew I was now truly alone.

I am Michael, and now I wish to tell a story of mercy, grace, and reconstruction of a life destroyed by my own hand. I have officiated three of my family's funerals and have given death rites to three out of four family members who have died since I've returned. But no, I am not death's angel, nor am I any sort of a spiritual giant.

Standing motionless and quietly beside that bed, I understood how all—and I do mean all—my life has led to this moment, and from henceforth, I would carry the responsibility of service to humankind for the rest of my life. It is written that someone once said, "There are two great moments in a person's life: the first is when they are born, and second is when they understand why."

I now understand.

I knelt, not to pray for Dad, for now he was beyond prayer and his peace had been made and it was only I that harnessed inner turmoil, but because I knew that his passing had become the catalyst for my path to continue. I prayed for myself. I prayed for guidance, prayed for strength that lay beyond me, and prayed about the welling fear seeping into my very bones.

I cannot tell you when the quiet prayer ended, but as the mind went about the business of attempting to balance sorrow and grief, I found myself catapulted back thirty years. Into the year 1990. The year in which I simply disappeared. Yes, walked off the grid of life because I couldn't exist among humankind. As an addict, alcoholic, and failure of a husband, father, son, brother, citizen, and everything else that humans are, I no longer had the wherewithal to sustain my miserable existence. Too afraid to live but also too afraid to die, I only considered the thought of going off and dying in the woods like the hunting dog that I was. I had shamed my family's name and embarrassed myself beyond belief, and I couldn't pull it together and saw no way out. Hopelessness, helplessness, and the darkening of my life had no other meaning except to calm the beasts of inner agony. In the grips of an addiction so bad that even when the sun rose I lived in darkness. With criminal intent, I scraped and conned enough money for a one-way ticket; that was all that I needed because I knew I would never return. Everybody was better off without me. And thus began ten more years of wanting to die, but breath kept me alive. How bittersweet these memories as they came to mind! And as they colored my head, I knew that one day I would have the strength to speak. I will try to tell of my journey and describe the anguish of a miserable soul losing and finding its way back into the ranks of humanity.

The following is only one of the many twists of my journey; perhaps it may provide some hope to you or those that may feel hopeless. Or this story line may be entertaining and grant some moments of self-reflection and to embrace all the varieties of living.

When most people honestly reflect upon their life, it becomes apparent that mistakes, mishaps, and wrong intents have played instrumental roles in the development of character and life circumstances. The accumulation and assessment of these events can and may be pondered. I have found that each individual is faced with the same basic questions, the variables of which are multiple: What do I want to do with my life? How do I get there? What do I need to do?

These are questions that are posed to us as children, adolescents, and young adults, even in our maturity and old age. Yet in the final analysis, the person must find revelation about what has been learned and what should be done to correct or alter the future progression of their lives. It is with this in mind that I now cast a tale of the moments of my own existence among the masses.

Is it truly possible to relay a lifetime of experience in any writing format? Stories, fiction or nonfiction, have always captivated the hearts, minds, and spirits of humankind since the development of a communication other than verbal. What do I wish to give to my reader that no other author has already rendered in the written word? It is my intention to give the reader my experiences in living color. Maybe a portion of emotions experienced during the various campaigns of my shattered life of disarray. I think what is about to unfold is nothing more than my experience. I hope to achieve some semblance of connection. Most of all, relieve me of the burden of shame, guilt, and remorse. Perhaps this will become the confessional tome to release the anguish of my soul.

Now, with all the introductions out of the way, let's get to know each other a tad bit better, shall we?

CHAPTER 2

The Changing of the Old

I t had been a few months since I had simply disappeared from my hometown. During my first days on the road, I encountered the first stages of homelessness in the USA. This stage was the learning of how to live in the streets. One had to develop an observational skill and get to know the ins and outs of each area that you traveled in. Readaptation to new circumstances was a must. Many mistakes, bad judgments, and frustrations came about. I had spent what small monies I originally had and any of the scrapings that I begged from any passersby. At this stage, the only thing that played in my favor was absolute ignorance! It is said that God protects little babies and fools. What I can tell you is that I was no little baby and I was an unadulterated fool, in the first degree. My days consisted of walking, thumbing rides, or placing distance from people who chased and pestered the homeless, just for kicks, and begging for any scraps I could get. I originally went south, and as the days grew in length, there was no specific direction I headed. Most of the time, I could find a bottle to drink myself into a numb state. After a day or two in an area, I would drain the bottle and spin it. This became my general compass for travel destination. Whatever direction the neck of the bottle pointed, that was the way of travel.

It's funny how after a short while on the road, time begins to occur not as we understand it but as conceptualized by activity. Instead of the clock or days of the week, or even the month, time becomes activity—time to move, time to eat, time to hustle/beg, time to bed down, and time to seek oblivion. Without instruction, I began to morph into the nether regions of human existence. Each day brought me closer to a primal self; it became instinctual instead of intellectual. Slowly, civilization seeped from me and aboriginal man began to emerge. The cold, heat, rain, and wind replaced my civilized concept of time. These elements dictated what should be done to ensure that my spartan needs were met. I inserted myself into the world below the watchful eye of society and entered into the belly of the beast.

For the most part, I traveled alone, though at times two or three of us would band together for a few days and pitch camp on city skirts or wooded areas. I learned quickly sometimes there's really no power in numbers and alone may be best. The bottle was spun while three of us discussed what were the future possibilities. Two of my companions talked about hitching up with a migrant camp that traveled the East Coast. They said we could start in Florida picking oranges, lemons. The route would lead us up the coast, changing with the season's growth. Peaches, tobacco, cucumbers, and farther north, we could do apples. What made it a possibility in my mind was that you got room and board and were paid. However, at that time I had already established that these men were just as untrustworthy as I and soon there would be a falling-out. My preference was not to have unnecessary conflict, and though companionship was good, this situation was heading toward a negative blowout. They headed north, and that left three other directions for me to choose. My decision was to head a few miles east to a town that had a railroad—perhaps I'd be lucky enough to get a boxcar shelter.

And luck was with me.

As I walked on the road, it was a beautiful day, not too hot; it was just right. Sometimes, no matter your condition, things are just right, and this is how I remember that day. I was able to get a ride, and the driver offered me some tokes off a joint and made small talk. Then he let me out about two miles from where I wanted to go. As I started toward a wooded area I had seen before, I decided to look for the rail tracks, and of course, I knew they would lead me to my new possible digs for a day or so. Up ahead, I heard machinery running and a chain saw buzzing and men shouting to one another. I walked toward the sound in the hopes I could pick up a few hours' labor. It appeared Lady Luck was still riding with me as I approached the group and said I'd be happy to work for a sip of water, food, and a couple of dollars. The man looked me over and said, "Sure." He said he would give me thirty dollars to help cut up wood and feed them to the wood-chipping machine and that, with my help, it could be done in about four hours. We were done in three hours, and though I can't remember their names, I know they were a great group of men. They took me to town, fed me, paid me forty dollars, got me drunk and high, then took me to the liquor store before dropping me outside the fence line of the railroad depot at about 9:00 p.m. They advised that the hole would be best to get in and shouldn't have a watchman come around until eleven thirty that night.

It didn't take me long, and once inside the yard, I found the ideal location on a third track, a boxcar not hooked to an engine—and it appeared not to have been used a while. I could tell it had been camped out in before, but not recently. I bedded toward the back, first taking a piece of steel that I found in the yard for a weapon, leaning it in the darkness within hand's reach. Once I had my security in place, I settled down for my one-man party of the bottle and the couple of weed roaches given to me. Man, this was the life!

CHAPTER 3 —————————

War and Choosing

Regaining the rudiments of consciousness after a night of again being in a drunken and drug-induced state of unconsciousness, I sensed a tumult of sounds invading my fogged mind. I rolled to one side in hopes of dislodging the constant buildup of phlegm in my sinuses and I hocked and regurgitated huge amounts of spittle and snot noisily. Afraid to shake my head to clear it, quite sure my brain would explode instead if I did, I simply tried to deep-breathe in the hopes that fresh oxygen would provide merciful relief. I attempted to kick-start my day, remembering where I was and how I got here, and whether or not I was with someone. These stupors were becoming more frequent. Later, I would learn that these memory lapses were blackouts.

As this running narrative was grinding through my mind, the pounding of my head increased, as it always did in my day after royal benders and upchucking previous night's poisons, followed by agonizing dry heaving into my morning ritual of coming into the land of the living. On my hands and knees, I heaved and sweated out, though the morning was cool. I knew from experience that I only had to hold very, very still and breathe. Soon the pounding would ease and dizziness would stop, and then I could move. Not fast, but slow and easylike. Indefinite moments dragged as I held my doglike position, on my hands and knees, afraid to move. "Just in and out, Mike, just in and out," I quietly whispered. Through my squinting eyes, I could see the birthing of the predawn hours, breaking the darkness of the night. Crawling toward the wall closest to the steel bar I had collected in the night when I'd come to the yard, I started hearing muffled sounds outside; however, I could not identify what they were—I really had my hands full with trying to get me together. This was the mother of all handovers, and I knew that I'd have to pay the devil in full, and the price was going to be steep. What I didn't know was that this was going to be the day when I would start to receive an education that would indeed save my life.

I made it to the supporting wall inside of the boxcar. I was alone, and sometime during the night, I had had the presence of mind for self-safety and had pulled the large door closed but had the inset man door ajar. As I craned my neck and back, the popping of joints seemed to ease the explosive headache I was nursing and started to quiet my rebellious stomach. Moving slowly, walking the length of the car and side to side, I began to feel better. I looked around, and by the gray light of morning I found evidence that this car had been used quite often. Some pictures of strangers, empty soda cans, food cans, condoms, and various pieces of clothing. I pissed in the back corner and decided to just lie awhile on the floor, now that I was fully conscious, and allow my mind to map out the day.

As I lay there with my head on my bag, the murmuring that I had picked up on during my morning near-death experience became a cacophony of the sounds of chaos. My misery was being invaded by the familiar sounds of battle. Twanging metal against metal, the thunking of wood against wood, feet scrambling and slipping on loose gravel. And then arose a sound in the midst of the muffled cursing and cries: this was the sound of metal mashing into flesh, and the thudding timber of dead trees assaulting human bodies.

I am not a stranger to violence, and at all costs, I needed to avoid any type of run-ins that may lead to arrest. When I left Pennsylvania, I also walked off two years of probation for carrying a firearm.

Underneath the rubble inside the rail car that I had sought refuge in the night before, I realized the encampment was under siege and the residents were being driven from the property. Judging from the noise, I could tell it was violent and swift.

As I gathered my meager possessions, my head went from a dull throbbing to an excruciating white light migraine. Leaning against the boxcar wall, I scanned my immediate area to see whether I had left any of my stash of liquor or weed. Of course, the best thing for a raging hangover would be aspirin, food, hydration, and rest— definitely not to start drinking again so soon. However, in a pinch like this, I decided that anything to dull the edge would have to do. I quickly rambled through my meager possessions, finding one old valium, about a half-pint of Thunderbird, and a roach clip-size joint, which were the savior for me. Intently listening to the outside ruckus, I knew that things had started near the entrance of the bunk yard and that it was systematically headed toward me. My plan was to evade and loop behind the crowd and then blend in with a hasty retreat. Now that the shakes and headache had given way to adrenaline rush, I started the action plan: I looked about for weapons. In this scenario, not knowing whom and how many I was up against, and not knowing enemies from friendlies, I had to have weapons that would not evoke obvious threat or fear. The metal piece would stay in the car; I could always fall back, as a last stand, to this spot. I chose the four-inch small assault wooden dowel and penknife that I always kept in my pockets. Then I laid my strategy down and began what I hoped to be an uneventful exit and disappearance.

I eased the man door insert open just a little and scanned my surroundings. For a few minutes, I watched several bands of tramps run past the boxcar, and I had sighted enough to count roughly thirty to forty people being chased and beaten by individuals in some type of paramilitary garb. Any direction that I turned, the same was happening throughout the yard. Once it was determined which direction would pose the least resistance to an escape, I eased out and gingerly hopped to the gravel stones around the tracks. That "gingerly hop" from the car jarred my dulled senses and almost made me puke. Breathing deep and slow, I listened in between the pounding of my head and the onslaught of the rampage about me. Of course, my hope remained that I be invisible; however, reality and the winds of fate had something else in mind!

I watched as groupings of men dressed in khaki uniforms, wielding clubs of metal, wood, and hard plastic, beat unmercifully at the trespassers. Stooping to look under the cars in the yard, I paused and scrambled behind a group of three or four tramps hightailing. I veered right around an engine that sat idling and quick-paced toward a small redbrick building. Once close enough to it, I rolled lightly on the ground close to the steps leading up to the porch and front door. Looking about and ensuring that I hadn't been seen, I hopped the railing on the side and inched toward one of the windows. Peering in, I saw a scattering of clothing, foodstuff, and bedding material. Quickly I surmised that this was one of the evicted shanties and knew it was time to keep saddling toward undetected escape. By now the surprised attack on the railway encampment had decreased in noise level, but the brutal eviction was still underway.

The scene unfurling before my eyes told of the true history of violence and how historically it had been practiced and perpetrated against one another in the name of self-justification. In all directions, the blur of motion and the agonizing sound of assault and pain misted the air. I have learned that it's best to first see the opposition and then determine the course of action, although this type of logic is only applicable in the art of war. But the scene clearly defined this as *war*; though it was lopsided and on domestic land, it was war nonetheless! The haves and the have-nots, the same old principle of who deserves the right to property and prestige, of who is beneath whom within the food chain.

Stooping in avoidance of detection, I began the crabbing bent loping, staying hidden among the yard scrap piles and debris. Groups of threes and fours of ragged men were battered by the policing brutes. These unfortunates were corralled toward a ragged hole in the outer chain-link fence. On the outside of this opening, men were stationed armed with sticks, clubs, and aluminum baseball bats obviously, a trap furthering the punishment for the trespassers.

Avoiding the bottleneck entrapment, I slipped around multiple Squawmish. Weaving under cars on the tracks and around post and huge heaps of old rail ties, for the most part, I was unseen. Occasionally, I would bump into one of the fleeing bums or I would dart toward the bottleneck, making it appear like if any of the would-be assailants saw me, then they wouldn't have had to pursue me, because I was already headed toward the trap!

Though my condition was not peak performance because I was still in the hangover state and I was sweating the liquor sweat of a drunk, for the most part my plan was working. I was heading in the opposite direction and, for all practical purposes, had broken into the freedom of daylight. Approximately three hundred yards and I could be out of the train yard, but I still had to be careful. Once or twice, I'd come across a few escapees and we'd scurry in different directions.

It was while crawling from underneath one of the cars that my luck played out. I had just stood up and turned to look behind me when, at the same time, two armed thugs rounded the back. At first, I ran, giving the appearance of being full of fear and of helplessness, and to act as the other sheep on the run. My pursuers seemed to get a great kick out of this; even though I was leading them to the bottleneck trap, they were more interested in attacking and hurting me. When I realized that they truly meant to harm me, not just to chase me from the premises, I changed my direction toward the tracks, which had cars to hide from what was about to go down. However, though I had given up hope in the land of the living, there was still the element of the warrior that remained alive. Once I found three tracks that had cars on them to block the view, I led my attackers to a blind spot. When I heard them turn the corner of the boxcar, I slowed my pace and dropped my carrying bag to the gravel and turned. This action brought them to a menacing slow walk toward me.

I called out, "Boss, I'm just trying to get up out of here."

That didn't do anything but make them laugh. One of them even said, "Nigga, you should've thought of that before you came in here. Naw, you gonna get yo Black ass whipped!"

As far as I was concerned, the line was clearly drawn in the sand now.

When a man, or should I say any human, had come to a place in their life such as I had come from, where nothing was worth living for, or there was nothing to be hoped for, and the only respite would be a merciful death, then for anyone to evoke anything other than despair would create an unexpected turn of events. It must be remembered that even a small mouse, when cornered, would likely turn and attack a ferocious lion!

I'm not going to go into details, because at this time, let's just say they did get some Black ass, but it wasn't what they thought or bargained for. It can be said that if indeed they lived, it was a day that they would never forget. It convinced my would-be assailants that perhaps a more compliant prey should have been selected.

My real intent was getting the hell out of Dodge as quickly as possible before someone sounded any alarms. Espying a route of least resistance, I started at a dead run.

Up until this moment, I had traveled the homeless road by myself. Most transients traveled in twos or threes for safety and resource finding and watching over acquired caches of foodstuff and other items deemed valuable but untransportable at the time. I traveled alone in self-misery, isolation, and residual despair, sometimes even anger, because of the encroaching fear that I would be another day in this hell. I wanted no companionship, no other responsibility but me. I had learned that in our imperfect state of human condition, we would fail one another at the most critical time, and further, we were unable to carry out even the smallest of tasks without the ability to complete it. Reflecting, I now know that this global labeling was then only applicable to me.

With this mindset, I avoided helping the injured and ignored the pleas for help or mercy. I wrapped myself in self-suffering, attempting to feel nothing for those who were being terrorized and brutalized. I made my way with deaf ears and blind sight through the one-sided battle, with only mild interruptions. Though I tried to stop the welling of what I had been trained to do, which was battle and stand for those who could not stand for themselves, I found that the self-imposed walls began to dissolve. So did my resolve not to help. Through the encampment of the rail yard, items like blood, paper, meager possessions, and clothing littered the ground. Avoiding the multiple Squawmish, I witnessed the carnage of human abuse and the stirring of dead dreams. My heart bled.

Though my conscience began to take hold, yes, I found that I was slowing down and noticing my heart screaming, "You must help!" Yet I stuck resolutely to my claim that none of this was my problem; thus, I continued to transverse the carnage.

Then it happened!

One moment, "Get the fuck out"; the next, "Enough is enough."

I am a man of spiritual belief; even in my days of darkness, I believed, not so much in fate, but actually in the God of the universe, Creator of all things. So what happened next, I know, was his design.

Coming from behind a caboose car, I could see that I was very close toward my exit point, which was a small hole in the ground, under the chain-link fence. The fence had been pulled up just enough that a body could crawl under. At the same time, as this thought of blessed freedom entered my mind, I came face-to-face with three assailants terrorizing an elderly tramp.

Drug addiction; alcoholism; failed marriages; dereliction of duty as a father, citizen, son, and/or brother; tossed careers; and a host of others more caused the imprisonment of my good self. However, there is one thing more that I must bring into the equation of my dismal self-circumstance. At that time back in 1991, I was thirty-three years of age, but at the age of six years old, I had already started my study of the Martial Way. I not only had attained the black belt ranking but also had excelled in two styles, one of which I held in second-degree, and my original style. I held six degrees. I believe that my surrender to substances and subsequent lifestyle demoralization was bad in itself; however, as a Bushido warrior gone to seed, I found it to be more than I could bear, so I simply quit living—actually, I died.

Dear readers, this is not a martial arts book, but to fully understand me, you must have certain intel. The moment that I came face-to-face with this scene, I could go no further with my escape plan. I understand that that moment defined the first "one of many" experiences that would lead me back to the true path of life. However, at that time, it was an "Aw, shit" moment.

An light-skinned elderly Black man was surrounded by three paramilitary-garbed White men. I didn't see race at that time because many of the droves that were driven out were Whites, Latinos, along with Blacks. Yet what I witnessed, elderly abuse and unnecessary abuse and one person being outnumbered, sickened me. What enraged me was that any one of the antagonists could have handled the suffering specimen by themselves, and yet this inhumane treatment appeared to be normal and acceptable to them.

Tauntingly, they kept him off-balance as they shoved and lightly kicked at him to ensure off-balancing. Herding him as an animal and cursing that he was nothing, and something about the world being better without people the likes of him.

Though I was an emotionally and spiritually hollow man, I became enraged. This was not the type of blind rage that some say they go "blank" in; no, this was the cold, calculating weapon of a seasoned warrior. I advance quietly, keeping my eye trained on the entire area and specifically making a note of what weapons they had. Fortunately, there were no guns to be seen, or even knives. Only one had a board approximately two or three feet in length; it was a two-by-two. He seemed to be the leader. The other two continued to shove and cackled as the old guy fell to the ground, then they would pick him up and start the entire process again as they hurled insults at him. On occasion, the ringleader would poke him with the end of the stick, just to make a point. It all seemed to be in slow motion as I advanced upon them.

When I got about five feet from them, their backs to me, I announced my presence in a growling, low, menacing voice: "Stop this." Two khaki-dressed men immediately turned at the sound of my voice from behind them, while one held on to the hapless old man by his ragged lapel. The closest, the ringleader of the trio, turned while simultaneously backhanding with a small club. At that moment, he and his companion understood that I was not helpless and hopeless. Neither was I merciful in his attempted bully maneuver. Seeing his comrade screaming from the ground, holding an obviously broken elbow, he left his prey, but not before kicking the old man in the upper thigh. I watched as he gauged the distance between us to time his forthcoming sucker punch. However, he was just a brute, and I a warrior. And I was pissed off. I heel-kicked him as he advanced, catching him in the sternum. With bulging eyes, he wheezed for breath, his knees buckling in slow motion, and then I spun with all my might in a spinning wheel kick with my right leg, connecting to his head.

The third assailant started throwing handfuls of gravel at me, screaming, "Damn you, boy, you done fucked up!" I quickly smacked him in the face with the board dropped by the ringleader. Fortunately, our tussle didn't sound any louder than the surrounding noises. However, I knew they'd be on me, because Mr. Board-in-Face was screaming and running to get help.

With no further delay, I ran to the slumped figure of the victim. He was dazed and had seen some of, if not all, the encounter. Quickly I asked if he could move, and he replied, "We'd better haul some ass." The loudness of the purge had somewhat been toned down; I could hear the loud-pitched sound of the man I hit with the board in the distance as brutes and prey continued the exile. I took the old man's satchel and helped him to his feet, then we headed toward the chain-link fences, which could accommodate our escape without further incidence. We reached the fence, and I decided to go through first; I clambered crab-like through the small opening near the ground. After I was through, I had him lie on the ground and place his arms through the opening, and I pulled him to the safety of the outside fence line. He immediately said to keep moving and that he could show me a place where we could rest. Half-carrying him and his meager possessions, I toiled under his directions. Instead of heading to the wooded area I had seen, he directed me toward town.

CHAPTER 4 ————————————

Alliance

It was still early in the morning. What I am saying is that all this began in the twilight, before the sun actually began to rise over the hills. The dew was still heavy on the grass, and a hazy fog could be seen in the deserted streets of the town. Though it gave the feeling that hours had passed, in actuality it was no more than forty to sixty minutes from start to finish.

After various twists and turns, up one street, down three streets, and through several yards, and passing soup line gatherings, the old man said, "Hold up." We had entered an alleyway that dead-ended at a brick wall and several dumpsters.

Looking around at the dead end, I quickly scanned the area that we had just passed through to ensure we weren't followed. I continued to wonder why he had said to stop; perhaps he was still disorientated, so I still supported his weight and didn't loosen my grip on him even though he had started to stand on his own. While carrying him, I did note that though he was thin, not skinny, he was strong and sinuous. I couldn't guess his age, but I knew he was at least two decades older than my thirty-three years of age. As I was holding him up firmly, he placed a steady hand on my arm and said, "Son, I'm all right. I can stand, and this is where we need to be." I believe that he said this because he noticed that I was still in fight-or-flight mode. Before letting him go, I searched his face, and looking into his eyes, I could tell he was present and accounted for. Simultaneously, I noticed that he took an assessment of me.

I loosened my supportive hold on my charge and allowed him to slump to the ground. Asking him to hold still, I began to assess him for bodily damage. While he submitted to this, he carefully watched me, and as I asked questions, probing, he answered each of my inquiries on his discomfort. After I was done with this rudimentary medical "checkup," he finally spoke. "Son, you don't belong here, but I'm glad you showed up when you did." Not really thinking of what he said, I asked him why we were in this alley. I was thinking that this was a bad position to be in. Also, why here? Especially since we had passed several soup lines to eat. He said, "Boy, we'll get better service here than there." Hearing him say this, and while looking at our present location, I turned and looked into his rum-lidded eyes just for that moment, and for whatever reason, I believed him. Though he was a drinker and, from what I could see, just another bum in the street, there was a presence about him. Not the type of air of forced power or fame, but a subtle influence of a wizen personage.

As if on cue, one of the metal doors clacked open and a short-order cook appeared in the doorway, jovially greeting the old bum. "Shoes, you were running late, so I just held some of the leftovers inside the warmer! I'll get 'em while you clear up the dumpster area again. Those no-accounts trashed it again."

"No problem, Greaser," was the old man's reply.

I was dumbfounded at this exchange and must have appeared stuck on stupid and parked in dumb, because the old man simply tugged at my sleeve and said, "Come on, boy," and led to one of the dumpsters that I had seen when turning into the alley after our escape. I looked back toward the alley entrance as the old guy headed to the three dumpsters, then I followed his lead. I began to pick up trash of all sorts, and there were moments I lost my appetite, because not all of it was typical refuse but human and animal compost.

Reflecting on that day, I realize it was my first dumpster experience, and it was just the beginning of one of many. Throughout my years in the wilds of America, I would find a home, battleground, and assignments concerning dumpsters. Thinking of this makes me smile, but believe me, at that time it was no smiling matter, and I couldn't imagine anything worse than the wafting scents. Little did I know that dumpster smells are not that bad and many times, going into new areas, you can learn a lot about a place by what's in the trash. However, at this time, what I was learning was that maybe I should rethink the direction of my choices!

Back at the open doorway, two five-gallon buckets of sudsy water had appeared. I looked questioningly at the man called Shoes—that was what I remembered the cook had called him—and yet again he discerned my questioning look. "Boy, a man can't eat lest he wash first, because we in the street, God knows we ain't animals, though most folk think so. After we wash, we eat, and then we brush down this door entrance for the day's business with this here water and broom."

Since my dropping off the earth several months before, the only thing I had done was drift. I had no plan or direction. My dereliction of societal contribution and participation was nil. I had stopped to think as a common human. My needs or wants were basic; in a relatively short time, I had gone from civilized to primal. This was in every sense of the word! So when this old man said that we were not animals and that we all wash before eating, this became my first lesson under his instruction. *Wow!*

Beside the buckets was a covered plastic tray, and under this cover were bacon, eggs, grits, Danish, and scraps of other meat and potatoes. Shoes said, "Boy, we put up those there potatoes and Danish because you never know when you get to eat again and it's best to have a stash in your bag." I watched him as he went into his bag and pulled plastic bags from it, and I did what I was told and rummaged in my bag until finding old plastic baggies / bread bags.

During the course of our feast, Shoes began to give me the basic lowdown of who he was in a general way and spoke about this road of life that I had entered. I do not remember him speaking of how he came about road life, nor did he reference the time that he had been on the road. I was impressed that his factual knowledge of the Depression era and recessive periods of American life had always moved some citizens in the shadows. He stated, with authority, that it was part of living and that it had always been that way. Shoes explained that this phenomenon was not only in America but also all over the world. He said he believed that if there were other worlds within the universe, there would always be subsocieties within major societies. How he painted the tramp world and the necessity for it made a lot of sense back then, and even now.

Never did he ask why I had come to the life on the street, and nor did he suggest my staying on the street or hightailing it back into mainstream society. Very simply, he accepted that my fate and reasoning were my own to make and the only thing that he could contribute would be about the things he had learned and the code of the street, or street law. Choice would always be mine and mine alone. I do remember this: "Boy, no matter how a man decides to live, in a shithouse or a mansion, live big or live small, his decisions always carry consequences. Now, whether the decisions are good or bad, it don't make no difference. What really makes the difference is whether the man is willing to live with the consequences of his decisions without bitching and thinking that someone else is supposed to shovel him out from the shit he created! That's just that simple." He said this in a finalizing statement with such certainty that I took it for the truth, and over the years I've often heard these words echo in my head. I believed them then, and I still believe it today.

Little did I understand that this man would become my mentor and a lasting living memory for the rest of my life. The half an hour of our dining versed me on why he was called Shoes and the way of street survival. Shoes came into the urban undertow years before; he did not give the details of the how and why, or even when. Throughout his discourse, I surmised it was indeed decades. In a matter-of-fact, monotone voice, he found that he could no longer live in society and took to the road. Even in my dumbfounded state, I knew better than to ask, so I just intently listened.

"There are classes of tramphood. You will find some that are temporarily homeless, down on their luck for one reason or another, but for the most part, many are able to shake the dust and return to what's normal. You have the junkies and drunks and criminals. Boy, you got to remember, for the most part, the problem is them trying to get their fixes or drink. This goes for the criminals as well. You can't really trust them, even though they are basically good people gone to seed. You always got to remember that when that monkey is on them, they'd steal Jesus off the cross then go back to steal the nails! Treat them like the sick people that they are, but you got to protect yourself from their sickness. They don't really mean no harm, but when you find your shit's gone, you gonna be mad and ain't no need to be mad at them, because you knew all along not to trust them. Now, boy, we got people that are sick in the head, some born that way and others made that way. It really ain't no way to tell the difference, but they are sick and can be dangerous, so you got to be careful with them. You never know when they might just do you harm, because they sick. Then you got them Bums, for the most part bums are a good bunch, but at any time they can turn into pack wolves. Normally they travel in packs of five or more. This is so they can go someplace to set up a camp and leave couple to guard the ground that they staked as their camp. For the most part, it be best to leave them alone. Don't go near their camp, not unless you're invited. Then, if you are, be careful, because sometimes they want to make sport of you."

I stopped him and asked what he meant by *sport*. In a matter-of-fact tone he said, "They don't normally keep women in the group because it causes too much hard feelings in the tribe that one is getting nooky and the others ain't, but it don't stop them from wanting it. So on occasion, they catch a newbie like you, make them feel welcome and homely and safe. As time goes on, the one that brought you in would try to own and make you pay for the safety and companionship. Most of the time, the newbie gives a little and takes a little. Sometimes the newbie just ain't bending, and that's when the real trouble starts. The newbie don't have the protection anymore, and the gang rapes him. Who's gonna care?"

Hearing this, I began to appraise the speaker's intent toward me. As if reading my mind, he said, "Boy, don't go stupid on me. I ain't got nothing for a man! Shit, it's been so long for a woman I probably forgot, besides pissing, what else I could use my pecker for!"

I nodded to let him know that I understood what he was saying, but I had already decided that if I was still with him by nightfall, he'd definitely fall asleep before I did, and then I'd sleep light, if at all.

Though we had finished our meal, he continued the session, as if it were important that I get the scoop of my predicament. Shoes spoke of the population of homeless just as though it were a school curriculum. I do not remember all of it; however, it came to a portion of information classified as the hobo. Hoboes are the upper class of all homeless individuals. They are the elite. When Shoes began his extrapolation of hobo hood, a glint and hint of pride let me know that I was in the company of an elite vagabond. The hobo is not at a disadvantage or a victim of hard times or down on his luck. It is by design that the man has chosen to shake off civilization and its petty ways for freedom of the road and the excitement of simple everydayness. The way in which he laid it all out it made perfect sense; one could only imagine why school hadn't had it as a course study!

Just like how in the standard social system with its different classes and democracy we find that any person with humility can overcome poverty, abuse, and mental or physiological challenges and become the elite of finances and affluence, so could any disenfranchised individual rise to the pristine society of "hoboism." From what I was able to understand from this diatribe, the type of commitment and drive needed from the individual targeting this coveted spot was indeed the same exact motivation needed in mainstream society. What I couldn't and didn't wrap my mind around was that if it took the same level of fortitude as the regular world, why be a hobo? Of course, I didn't speak this sentiment; I was just a listening audience. However, even in my infantile state of being streetwise, I knew his information would prove to be valuable.

During his discourse, I sat across from him as he sat on the stoop of the doorway, and I on the ground, facing him. I watched as his eyes took on the "far back in the day memory" look. I was fascinated by what I was seeing and held captive by his wave of stories, which held emotions, and the inflection, brought to life by his voice, and the serious and trivial importance of the information given. I could almost identify at what age different things had come about in his life. It appeared that as he spoke about the routes he had traveled, his physical appearance changed, sometimes childlike, other times youthful, and still at others mature, and still at other more times old, much older than his present years. It was amazing. I watched him morph into the present moment and knew that this session would be over momentarily.

He shook himself loose from his history lesson and stated we'd better get to moving, that there were things that needed to be done in order that we'd have a place to sleep tonight. I was wondering where I would rest for the night, being that my roost had been busted. I knew that he had mentioned that so that it was both an invite and a suggestion that wherever we bedded down, it should be together, at least for this night. With gratitude that at least one of my necessary basics was covered, I dismissed it from my mind and set to the task at hand.

Gathering the remnants of our meal and bagging leftovers in our bags, we began the chores of cleaning and washing down the door entrance and sidewalk. All the while my mind raced and thought on the things that were said. Shoes went about the task with practiced skill and spoke little. After the early-morning rousting in the rail yard, he was sore and stiff in some of his movements, and at those instances, I'd silently lend a hand. At each hand lending, he would emphasize the need to pay attention to certain details and give instructions when none were needed. A couple of times I caught him out of the side of my eyes watching and chuckling to himself as he watched me, shaking his head slowly. He told me to knock on the door but not enter, and the cook to give us a couple more buckets of clear water to rinse away the debris. When the job was completed, he said to leave the buckets and broom by the door; the cook would get them.

As we picked up our bags and secured them, we headed toward the alley entrance. While the morning sun had risen enough to start to warm the day, it was comfortably cool. Once at the opening, he said that the first thing we had to do was to make some rounds to find out if anybody was seriously injured and needed some doctoring, and to find out whether or not the town was really purging the riffraff again. Of course, that statement piqued my interest, and I had to ask what he meant, because what I had witnessed in the morning hours definitely meant to get out and not come back! While we walked slowly onto the main drag, he began to explain the politics of road life.

"Sometimes, normally in elections, with bigwigs passing through, or a town trying to get more money, they would first run off all the undesirables so that whatever powers that be may come to look into the requesting party's area, they wouldn't see vagrants polluting the scene. In other words, they wanted the place to look presentable and that it would look better if they had more spending money to spruce it up." Also, he made it a point to tell me that even the head busters at the rail yard were just doing their job, and to never be angry at a man for doing his job. He said, "It's like cops and a robber. The job of the robber is to steal and take what ain't his to take claim on. The cop's job is to catch the robber. Most people believe that cops are there to protect the community and to serve. In fact, that's how it appears. But the truth of the matter is that it's just a job. Those head busters, for the most part, are pretty good Joes, sometimes even joining in on a drink now and again."

Now, that statement took me for a loop as I thought about those men that had him this morning. But I kept all that to myself.

"Now, boy, there are some that got mean streaks, maybe because of what someone had done to them, that makes them want to hurt others. This gives them the legal opportunity to do it. All that yelling, cussing, and dust are for show. Believe it or not, even the yelling from the bums is for show!"

Now, I couldn't keep the surprise of this statement from my face, and I couldn't help myself from saying, "What the hell are you saying? I was there and saw that with my own eyes and heard it with my ears. That blood looked real to me!"

"Boy, I ain't saying that some of it was not for real! What I am saying is that it was a ruse—we knew about it!"

I stopped and looked at him, but before I could say a word, he stopped and began to explain.

"Boy, what you did was real, and that's what you be needing to know."

With that, his moment of pause ceased and he began walking toward the depths of town, with me in tow.

As I walked with him, I digested this information, not really understanding any of it, and thought about our morning meeting and how it looked very real to me as I saw the rips in his thin clothing, the bruised lip, the abrasions on his hands, and the limping gait. Finally, I told myself, what I did was just for show too.

We walked in silence. He led, and like a lamb to slaughter, I followed. Up ahead, slowly the town started to come to life as workers passed us, walking, driving, and busing to unknown workplaces. Occasional greetings to Shoes came from a variety of people. This astounded me; people from the real world, heading to work or bustling in the appearance of taking care of some type of business, actually acknowledged this hobo as if he was human!

All around me, I kept getting a feeling that I could not name. I continued to mull over all that had occurred in the early-morning hours and how now, seeing the awakening town come to life, I was amazed at the fact that no one appeared to be affected by the brutality and the fate of the disadvantaged population. Slowly I became aware of the persistent feeling that had been growing in my gut: it was invisibility! I could see the haggard look of last night's party on the man driving the UPS truck; additionally, I was looking into the eyes of a woman that were vacant for some unknown reason. I could see clearly, but to them, all of them whom we passed by, I was nonexistent. This was the first of my many awakenings on the road.

Not only had I ceased to be human, but society had also erased my presence from their reality. This did not pain me, however, because of my acceptance of my condition.

Today, as I write of these things, I am certain, though I was unable to verbalize this coincidental happenstance of events that led to my meeting my mentor, Shoes, I know today nothing about that phase of my life was by chance—it was destiny! This is not a story about religion; however, it is a story about some things that cannot be explained and are, within themselves, spiritual in nature and are, indeed, unexplainable truths. So believe what you will and I'll tell it as I experienced it, to the best of my ability.

One thing was quite obvious: my initiation and training for life on the road had begun. Up until this morning, I was a bumbling tramp, drifting anywhere, at any time. This kind and seasoned man took me, unbeknownst to myself at that time, under his wing. Perhaps this was his way of giving back something to a world that ceased to exist for him long ago. Or it could have been a passing of his legacy so that, as with all things, it/he might live, not only in memory, but also in the actual moment of the now. Whatever his reason, I will never know, nor do I think it important to. As a subject for discussion, this is the major point: Shoes provided the guidance and love that would not only ensure my survival but also afforded me the opportunity to thrive and learn to live again in the land of the living. For this, I am grateful and humbled by this benefactor's action of compassion in a time of fateful circumstances.

As we continued our walking, Shoes would stop and speak to one or two displaced people. I stood by silently as he conferenced. I was still mesmerized by a system overload of new emotions that were yet unidentified, and as I watched the frequent interactions of my newfound savior, my eyes and head began to hurt. I asked Shoes if I could meet up with him a little later, saying that I needed to get myself together. He looked steadily at me, as if evaluating a trauma victim, and agreed that there were a few more places he needed to check. Additionally, he stated that there was a park nearby and gave me directions, saying that he'd send someone for me in about an hour. If no one came for me, then we agreed to meet at the corner where the soup line began about four o'clock that evening.

Park Reflections

As we parted company, I saw that Shoes flagged the driver of an old pickup truck and got into the truck's bed and was driven eastbound toward an unknown destination. I was certain that we'd meet at the designated time. Still, I was somewhat amazed that it appeared the townsfolk knew him and had some type of agreement of his presence among humankind. I stood and looked about me and decided, instead of heading directly to the park, I would first head farther into the town for my personal look about without interference. Being that the railroad yard was located on the outskirts of town, I knew that I'd be able to get a better perspective of the community's general attitude inside the town's city limits. With this information, I would be afforded the opportunity to plan a strategy of how I would be able to coexist with others without friction and drawing attention to myself. Even though it had been just a few months since my venture into the world of homelessness, I had gathered essential information through a hard-won experience: do not draw attention to yourself. One must learn to mix with the crowd, flow with it, and not become the target of vigilantes or the law. Though the homeless existence has many within its ranks, it is a lonely and hard, unforgiving life. I found that the loneliness I felt was derived from my own personal pain of remorse and my regrets on past choices, mistakes, lost opportunities, and present moments, all wrapped into a bundle of the constant ache of absolute relentless misery. There are no vacations from this wilderness of constant movement. Therefore, each must seek sabbaticals in small measures at every opportune moment to ensure strength throughout this nomadic journey.

With determination to head east because Shoes went west, I figured eventually he would tell me what lay in the west. I cut my course. Walking on the sidewalk, I looked into shop windows, seeing sundry items of commerce. Fruit stands in open-air markets, several butcher shops, and two small movie theaters. In short, this was what some would refer to as a quaint small town. The absence of a mall was notable, though a Kentucky Fried Chicken filled the air with the aromas of fried chicken and, of course, a McDonald's golden arch stood in the distance. Several school buses passed, with rowdy children aboard, and the occasional prowling vehicle of law enforcement made police presence noticeable. Walking at a slow-enough pace to not be labeled as a vagrant or a suspicious character, I passed two public parks that contained statues of long-past-dead founding fathers. What I was seeking was a refuge not close to the immediate central park area but close enough for me not to appear to be a stalker or pervert. Coming to the specific park that Shoes had directed me, I immediately knew that this would fit my most immediate need of quietude. I really had to give it to that old bird—he picked an excellent spot! It's really amazing the logistics that must be incorporated in everything that you do when your net worth is "homelessness." I found a strategic spot close to an outcropping of trees, easily seen from the main park, away from the shrubbery path, to avoid the appearance of concealment and be watchful of the comings and goings of the public. The ideal place, where, if seen by others, I would appear as an upright citizen sitting and enjoying the waning summer season, reading a book in quietude.

Checking the ground first for animal droppings and for insect infestation, I reached into my "sidesaddle" (book bag or carrying case for belongings) and withdrew a heavy shirt to cover the area that I'd seat myself on, leaning on the tree trunk.

Once seated, I unlaced my shoes and began to pull them off to adjust my socks, but then decided to do full honors to my feet, since this was the second day straight of wearing my shoes. So I set about the task of personal grooming. Pulling my one boot off let me know that I had made the right decision. As the cool morning air hit the outer sock, I breathed a sigh of relief. I pulled off the other boot, with the same effect. Wiggling my toes within my socks, I constantly kept watch of my surroundings. On more than one occasion, I had to move quickly and had lost a shoe or, even worse, a pair of socks during a retreat. Believe it or not, socks are one of the greatest bartering commodities; after all, a tramp's primary mode of transportation are their feet! Therefore, feet are to be kept in good running condition.

While the coolness circulated, I massaged both my feet gently with my socks on. Actually, I was blindly checking for any soreness, which might indicate blistering. I did note several discomforts on both feet. Before removing my socks, I rifled through my bag for the things I would need: a baggie of baking soda, salt, paper towels. Maybe if I had it, a prepackaged wet towelette and another pair of socks. It didn't matter whether they were clean or not. Staying watchful, I began to peel the material from my right foot. I wiggled my toes simultaneously, all the while hoping that skin wasn't being peeled as well. You can't imagine that to perform hygiene, even at a basic level, is a chore while on the road. As I eased the sock over the heel and down, the smell was as you can imagine but must be ignored. With a final tug, my right foot was fully exposed. Somewhat water-wrinkled because of sweat and, of course, water, it looked two to three shades lighter than me, had lint covering on it, and had dead skin accumulation between the toes. No description can define just how good it felt to have fresh air on that dog!

Gingerly removing the other, I sat for a few moments and allowed the air to circulate over my recently imprisoned feet, wiggling my toes and flexing them. I then began to visually inspect them one at a time, noting sore spots and sighting blisters. The first thing I did before doctoring them was turning the socks inside out and slapping them vigorously against my hands to dislodge dead skin and loose debris from them. Then I inspected each for worn, thin spots, burrs, or twigs. After, I began the cleaning. First, in between each of my toes, ensuring dead, loose, and callous skin was rubbed, not to the point of bleeding, but as clean as I could get it. After, I peeled and picked and rubbed so that smoothness was pretty much even over the entire foot.

The next stage was going to be a bitch.

I then took the baking soda and dumped a small mound into my hand and, at first, patted each foot, paying particular attention to between the toes and the blistered areas. It burned like the dickens, but this was crucial to treatment. A few moments later, I took my salt packets out and began to rub salt all over the areas I had done treating with the baking soda. People, I can tell you this type of self-torture is not for the faint of heart!

Two things to remember here: The baking soda serves a twofold purpose, absorbing moisture and neutralizing odor. Salt acts as both an astringent, meaning it helps in clotting, and a cleanser, providing some cleansing but also helping in the toughening of skin.

After a period of self-cursing and torture, I was done and my feet looked and felt as though they'd live to fight another day. I looked and saw that my socks had had enough time to air-dry into a stiffness that only dirty socks can do, but hey, they'd worked hard to be stiff! Putting away my supplies, I decided to place these socks into my bag of baking soda until I could wash them, or at least rinse them. With them inside the soda container, at least I wouldn't have the smell wafting from my bag.

Hygiene done, I extended my legs and settled with my back against the tree and stayed watchful of various pedestrians. It's kind of a strange phenomenon. Pedestrians can stop and look at you; however, if you look back at them, they perceive you as a threat, and before you know it, here comes the law. It becomes a skilled art form to be able to look back at someone and not elicit a fear factor as a potential threat. The adrenaline rush of this morning, a pretty good breakfast and meeting up Shoes, and completing medical treatment of my feet had taken a toll on my abused body. I tilted my ball cap forward to shade my eyes from the rising sun, in the hopes of catching a few winks of shut-eye undisturbed. Quietly I inhaled a slow, deep breath, held it, and then slowly released it. After doing a complete cycle of three, I settled in. Lightly dozing, I began to slip into the space of slumber, just between asleep and awake. I could hear the sounds of passing traffic, bits and pieces of conversations, crickets, birds, and the occasional scampering of small animals within the brush. With the gentle caress of the waning summer breeze, I slumbered.

In this dream state I could see myself at the window, peering from the concealment of a ragged curtain. Through the dirty panes of glass I stared at the house that I grew up in, with a stirring longing. I don't know how long I was standing in that spot of concealment, but I knew that guilt and shame were my constant companions. In time I would find that the "four horsemen" described in Alcoholics Anonymous literature would describe the haunting specters better than I could. Terror, bewilderment, frustration, and despair would be the denizens of my life. With me rooted and haunted in that spot, as if on cue in a movie, my mother came out of the front door of the house to smoke a cigarette. She was wearing the light trench coat that the family had teased her to no end about, reminding her how much she looked like the cartoon character Inspector Gadget. I smiled quietly through my turmoil as I watched her standing and looking about at the trees and road, turning this way and that, surveying all directions. To an onlooker, for all practical purposes, she appeared to be a causal smoker; however, I knew in my heart of hearts that she was looking for me. It was close to two months since she had last seen me in our small hometown. My shame and guilt, I couldn't hide from, but I could hide me from the look in her eyes. My profound sadness and shame took ahold of me, and I melted into the abyss of the dark night of my soul. The substance of the moment encased me. She who had birthed me was grieving for the lost child that I had become. Addiction, alcoholism, and criminal behavior had guided me onto a path that none could help me recover from. I knew no way out. Tears welled into my eyes as I heard the droning voice of my cousin continuing in the background, speaking to a coconut with a carved face that he called Mr. Coconut. Dropping the ragged draping into place, I had a foreboding feeling of impending doom. Death, I thought, would be better than this existence of a living dead.

This scene would play many, many times throughout the years, without relenting in its intensity. I did not know that that would be the last time I would see my mother alive, and her death would not be known to me until seven years after her burial.

Weighted emotions began leveling in my body, and alarms so loud ricocheted within my head. I was being pulled to the ground, my strength being replaced by multiple tremors of earthquakes. Falling to my knees, I could sense my breath only coming through shallow wisps of inhalations. My cousin, in a drunken and drug-induced focus, never stopped his dialogue with Mr. Coconut; it droned on and on. *I can't breathe,* I thought. *Let me die!* Vertigo slowly began its spiral into an unknown vortex. This shimmering scene fading as I succumbed to the void, I heard a sound much like that of a large flat stone being thrown into a pond. It was at this point that I ceased to fight; I welcomed the end of the road. *If this is death, I will embrace it!* I mused.

At that moment, in visceral clarity, my feet were being jarred over and over. I was being pulled back into real time. Intervals of being jarred or struck disturbed this quiet moment of surrender. Again, again the jarring, the knocking. The disturbance could and would not be ignored. Similar to the sound of rolling thunder in the distance. "Boy! Hey, boy." Again, the jolting of my lower extremities, and a little more clearly I could hear, "Damn it, boy, get up! Come on, get up!" Swimming from the depths, I slowly ascended toward the surface of consciousness, and still I heard my cousin's voice speaking to Mr. Coconut. Couldn't he just shut up?

CHAPTER 6

Digger

As I opened my eyes slowly, I could see a tramp, an older man, standing before me with both the look of concern and anxious anger on his face. Immediately, upon seeing me awake, he said, "Fool, get yo ass up! Can't be sleeping in da park! Jonny Law just waiting to lock any of us up!"

"Here," he said as he turned away from me. "Shoes says you be needing these trail busters." From his shopping cart, which came into focus in my fogged head, he rummaged through its contents a moment and tossed me a pair of shoes; they were actually some type of work boot, and later I'd be calling these brogans. They were worn, but not worn-out. Looking at my sneakers, even in my state of mind, I knew this was better than the invention of sliced bread! He also tossed me a pair of socks, having seen my naked feet. Like the shoes, they were used, but usable. I might add that one was gray and the other a dingy white, but socks nonetheless!

While I inspected my newly acquired wardrobe, the stranger continued his message errand service. "Shoes sez to make sure ya at dat corner by three thirty. He be right along 'bout that time. And don't talk to nobody!"

Before I could say thanks or really make out exactly what he said, he had rearranged his cart items and was already wobbly wheeling down the sidewalk without another word.

Placing my newly acquired commodities on my feet, and with one shoe in hand, one shoe off, I watched the messenger stop at a few of the trash receptacles and gather items to add to his shopping cart. Amazingly, it was just as natural as rain as he inspected the possible future of proffered items with the eye of a seasoned shopper. The sun was gently warming the morning air, and the ground mist was abating into a clear view. I thought to myself how many things had happened and how quick it had all occurred, and I estimated that it was only ten thirty in the morning! If things happened this fast always for the nomads, no wonder they looked so old and worn! An immediate rushing thought came to mind: *What would I begin to look like if I stayed on the streets?* Little did I know that fifteen years would accumulate before I departed the humble and dangerous road of the hobo. This is truly one of many times that I can say, "If I only knew then what I know now!" Yet just saying this is moot, simply because it took as long as it took for me to find reason to re-embrace life.

Coming to my senses and committing to moving from my resting spot before trouble came knocking, I opened the baggie of baking soda that contained the old socks. Wetting my fingers, I placed them in the baggie and started to finger-brush my teeth, tongue, and mouth. Then I swished my mouth vigorously with my own spit, then gargled and spit the salty solution at the base of the tree where I sat. Pulling a rag from my pocket, I spit at it repeatedly until it was sufficiently wet, then I began to wipe my face. I paid particular attention to around my eyes and nose to ensure that none of the rat curds gathered around the corner of my eyes and dried snot wasn't in my nose to gross anyone out. This morning ritual completed, I then began to gather my strewn items and rearranged my bag's contents. All the while, I continued to watch the town come to life as the morning marched on.

I took a few deep, calming breaths, retying my shoelaces, and got to my feet. I stomped softly, one foot at a time, to get the feel of the shoes. Satisfied with the tightness of the tied laces, I took several test steps and found, to my delight, that the wornness of the shoes had softened them to the point of comfort. However, for those who have never worn other people's shoes, you may find that not only do the heel and soles wear but the inside also conforms to the wearer's specific stepping stride and gait. I could instantly tell that the predecessor of this pair walked somewhat evenly and was sure-footed. The owner also cared for the shoes, keeping them clean and odor-free.

While standing, I was able to get a better look of my surroundings. The small rest had invigorated me to the point of orientation of where I was in reference to the rail yard, of the alleyway, and I could see various signs. I distinguished a larger street and assumed that it was some type of main street, one that many streets intersected, and with the decision to follow it, I set off.

Walking at a casual pace, I saw that this town looked like a mom-and-pop town, one in which everyone knew everyone and probably knew what one another did behind closed doors. This realization also set my self-preservation alarms off loud and clear. News would carry fast in this place, and I knew what had happened in the rail yard would be part of the morning whisperings. I was the proverbial bull in a china shop. A stranger, a vagrant, Black and alone! I had to find just enough concealment to blend, and right at this moment, I was definitely the fly in the buttermilk. Zigzagging from street to street and turning at random corners, I passed car detailing shops, restaurants, flower shops, and it appeared, every kind of religious church there was. Some of the pedestrians even greeted me with "Good mornings." I practiced my best social skills of less eye contact and only speaking when spoken to and keeping my moving pace, no matter how nervous I might be, at the same speed as the regulars. I had continued this patterned type of walk close to an hour when I came to a small old-type gas station. It had an old Texaco sign, which had seen better days, and pumps that still had glass heads on them, where you could see the gas before it pumped into your tank. While I watched these ancient pumps work, I spied a water spigot on the side. I decided to take a chance and went in to ask the clerk if it was okay to drink from it. I was given the okay. I hadn't realized just how thirsty I was. Easing around the side of the building, I peed quickly and started my time-wasting walk until my four o'clock meetup with Shoes. I had already circled the destination from several different routes to be sure that I knew where it was and decided to float around until then. The thought had even crossed my mind just to walk right out of town and be on my way. It was still early enough to find another night nesting site. God knows it beat just waiting around for someone to recognize you as one of the tramps that had caused harm to some officials! As this thought, along with other endless thoughts, passed through my mind, I continued to meander and sightsee without seeing.

In a few blocks I came to the intersection of Hobbs and Vine. Making a right turn, I caught sight of the familiar shopping cart of the messenger and shoe deliverer. I stood not on the corner but about midblock across from a small construction site. Trying to locate the owner of the cart, I began to see what looked like dust whirls drifting up from the inside of the dumpster. As I continued to watch the large construction dumpster, I could make out that things were being tossed out of it. "Well, if that don't beat all!" I said to myself. My curiosity got the best of me, and I decided to go have a look.

Crossing the street, I was able to occasionally catch a glimpse of a head, a hand, and tossed treasures as they were hurled from inside. At this range, I could hear the muffled sounds of self-talk and the rattle of debris being moved around. Being that I had seen items getting tossed, I avoided the targeted pile outside, fearing I might get my head busted. So I went to the opposite end and began to climb high enough just to see in. I could hear his murmuring curses and the sound of his unsteady step over debris within. Every now and then I could hear that all activity would cease, for an instance, and then hear an "Ahhhh" sound. Climbing onto the side to peer inside, I saw him unscrew a small bottle of grape soda and swig deep, gulping swallows, then, recapping, stowed it in the back pocket of his pants, which were too large. Yes, this was that "Ahhhhh" of a smooth drink. The waist of the pants was cinched tightly around his small frame to the extent that the material had gathered, making him appear as a starving artist, not that I had ever seen a starving artist; however, I am certain that the portraits, placed side by side, would be close if compared.

I said, "Excuse me, sir." In hindsight, I think I could have chosen a better approach, but of course, hindsight is always twenty-twenty! I damn near scared him to death! Truth be known, his reaction almost scared me to death! However, this was the approach, and this was what happened. Whirling around as if being shot, he tried to locate me by sound. When he was able to get his bearing and located and recognized me, he said, "Hell, boy! What ya want, boy?" It was not my intent to scare him, but the damage was already done. I had to really work from the backfield if I were to get on his good side, so this was what I said. "I…I…I was just wondering what type of place this was," I meekly replied. Well, that might not have been the best approach, because that question started a sling of curses and unintelligible gibberish and physical estuations that made me want to crawl into the nearest hole! What spewed from this old man was a series of sentences that ran without any punctuation!

"What ya mean by what type of place this is? Ya must be stupid! Ya too dumb to be a tramp, sho' 'nuff! No wonder Shoes don't want you talking to no one—you too dumb to talk!" Having said all that he said, as fast as he could, he stumbled back a few steps as if to make a point and reached for his grape drink bottle, unscrewed the lid, and took a shallow swig. He stood defiantly in the middle of that dumpster like the king of the hill.

I must have looked as stupid as I felt as I wrestled with his verbal assault; he stood challengingly, glaring into my eyes with embers of fire in his. Then the most unusual thing happened: he burst out in a roar of laughter! At that time, I was able to take the full measure of the bearer of the gifts of shoes and socks. Here was a man thin as the rails that we had been evicted from. Though he was thin by my standards, dressed in thread-worn green maintenance shirt and pants. He stood howling as if someone had told him the world's funniest joke, with a floppy hat a little too large for his head and an overly large brown trench coat that had died but not buried and some worn-out military boots. Around his neck was a mass of chains and trinkets. He laughed so hard he began to cough, which led to a hacking that ended with him almost choking. Coughing and gagging, he bent forward to try to catch his breath and, in return, started to hock the loose, rattling phlegm in his throat. Stumbling over the discards in the dumpster, he made his way toward the back side of it and began to hack, choke, and spit the slimed insides out of the dumpster's edge. I watched this horrid episode, spellbound. I really hoped that he wouldn't drop dead! After a few moments, he seemed to get himself together, and wiping his mouth and nose with the sleeve of his coat, he erected himself and turned once again to face me.

When he finally faced me and saw that I had witnessed this spectacle, he burst into another round of killing laughter, but this time he laughed so hard the tears would not stop running down his creviced face. This second bout of comic relief was so contagious that I started to chuckle at the mere sight of him trying to collect himself to finish cussing me for scaring him. That chuckle just opened the door for me to join in, like the joke was on someone else other than me. I can only imagine what anyone would have thought about the two us howling like two banshees in the dumpster; it goes without saying being inconspicuous was out the window! I understood at that moment that I had frightfully startled him, and this was his defensive move to cover what he considered to be a momentary lapse of control. This was also coupled with the fact that I must have looked just as scared and stupid! It had been a while since I laughed a deep, belly-aching laugh. We cackled and howled until tears streamed from our eyes, and trying to regain some dignified composure then, we'd be seized with another bout of delirium. What the hell was so funny then, I cannot tell you today. What I do know is that laughter becomes the healing ambrosia on the way of the road. Sometimes it is the only glue that keeps the mind from being lost when the vagabond wandering becomes too much.

After our guffawing laughter, giggling, and snorts abated, I cautiously rephrased my original question, ensuring that I made no sudden move or used a disrespectful tone of voice. I said, "Sir, I just got into town and was hoping that you could give me some pointers on how not to get into any trouble or draw any suspicions until I move on."

Scratching his butt and then adjusting his worn floppy hat, he said, "Well, the first thing I would suggest is to get in this dumpster and give me a hand with some of this stuff. The second, to stop looking like some pervert staring into a damn dumpster! Besides, I can't be climbing in and out of this box all day! And make sure not to sneak up on people!" Though he didn't answer my question directly,

I knew that he had consented to help me, if I was willing to help him. This would be my first of many dumpster diving experiences.

Never having really climbed into a dumpster to hunt for treasure, I had to find the proper toeholds and grips. Clambering up the side and heaving over the top, landing like the amateur that I was into the debris, I slipped and landed quite comically on my ass, with a short slide down on an old sheet of plywood. This solicited another roar of laughter from my would-be information source. I didn't join in this time, however, embarrassed, but more importantly, it was because I was quite seriously attempting to locate the splinters in my right ass cheek from the recent slide. Digging inside the waistband and back side of my pants, I automatically began to unbuckle my pants for some deep searching of the wooden assassins. During this search-and-seizure mission, the gaunt figure howled in laughter while I made monkey with myself finding slithers of wood. After an indeterminable amount of time, satisfied that I would live and, for the present time, have no more immediate discomfort, I asked him if he was ready to go back to foraging. Standing somewhat unsteadily, he could only nod while still snickering.

Making my way to him, I saw where he had piled debris in an area where he could isolate items to determine whether they were useful or sellable. I just began by his side, and without words we kept clearing a space large enough, which could be our catch pile. A *catch pile*, he explained, is made inside of a space of debris or trash, the reason for which is simple: you cannot carry all your stuff at one time, so you'll carry several small stuff and then return for the others. However, if your catch pile is exposed, it becomes the property of anyone who sees it; if it's camouflaged with other trash and debris, more than likely, you'll be able to reap your benefits. Yet catch piles are open game on the streets, so you must be fast and crafty. Of course, you got to try to find out what day they are dumping the dumpster—ain't no good to be in one of these then, for you could get hurt or killed.

We separated electrical wire, glass, plastic, various lengths of rope, and he had me pick up nails and screws and place them in a pile. Throughout the morning hours, we worked silently. Occasionally, he called out, "Hey, boy, take a look at this!" On more than one occasion, he'd explain the reason that the hunt was going so well or going to hell. During this scavenger hunt, we both said little, though my mind continually ran through previous, current, and possible future occurrences at rapid speed. I felt it better to allow the process to play out at its own pace. I'm guessing around the noon hour he announced that we'd better get some lunch and hightail it back here to pick up our booty if we expected any pay for our treasure hunt. Though I didn't say anything, I did note that he said "we" when speaking of getting paid. We climbed out on the farthest side from the street, hidden from the casual eyes of the townspeople. Before leaving, he had me cover the catch pile with worthless debris, and then we climbed out of the dumpster.

Brushing himself and readjusting his too-large-fitting clothing, he pointed and said, "Come on, boy." And off we went!

Cutting through alleyways, streets, and an occasional backyard, we went at a quick pace toward our destination. As I was traveling with this man, my mind really wasn't on where we were going, or even meeting up with Shoes, but on what was really going on that every time someone referred to me, it was *boy*. In that single morning, I had been called boy more times than when I was an actual boy child! Yet though I was taking offense to what was not offending, I thought I had just cause to demand respect. But reflecting on this today, I know with certainty, believe it or not, it was a simple term of endearment when an elder of the road recognized that one needed help, even if one didn't know it themselves. I fell into this latter category.

CHAPTER 7

Lunch at the Asylum

We arrived at a Salvation Army soup kitchen. The line was already halfway up the block. We stopped by the entrance and were given a numbered meal ticket and then headed to the back of the line. Passing the waiting people, I noticed some were seated on the sidewalk on duffel bags, others on crutches and wheelchairs, and most stood with vacant stares, even engaging in superficial conversations. There was an odor that permeated from the crowd; it was notable at the entrance, though it was masked with cleaning product and antiseptic fragrance. I will not state the obvious of unwashed bodies and foreign remnants of previous dumpster dives, but as I am aware, there are certain sounds, sights, feelings, and yes, smells associated with scorn and shame. The end result of so many people gathered in despair creates a toxic aroma of pending death. It becomes the pungent odor associated with a dead mouse caught in the trap and not found until days later. Over time, if one continues to stay on the road, this smell becomes the norm of our everydayness. All this cascaded my already-overloaded mind as we took our waiting position to be admitted and fed, just one of the many castaways washed onto the shores of isolation.

Up until he offered his hand and said, "Boy, my name is Digger," I had not thought to ask his name, lest I break some unspoken code. These words invaded the space of my ongoing thoughts. For a moment, I had left the present and had gone to the library inside of me to catalog and reference all that had happen so far, so the interruption was a teaching moment to remind me to stay focused on the here and now, at least until it was a more appropriate time to analyze. I, without thinking, said, "I'm Michael." Immediate rebuttal from Digger was, "Don't matter. Glad to meet you." Again, I felt that he had insulted me. I held my tongue and contained my emotional disturbance.

He extended his hand, which I shook, and, as an afterthought, gave a grimacing scowl as a smile, self-conscious of his missing teeth. As we stood awaiting the movement of the line, Digger started to talk. The gist of our conversation was this: "Boy, you saved ole Shoes's ass back in that yard. From what he said, you be some kind of karate man. Don't matter. Shoes say you part of us, and, boy, he said you ain't got sense 'bout street life but you can make that up 'cause you a fighter!" I understood what was being relayed to me were several things at once: One, that this Shoes had some type of respect on the street community and to do for or against him was to be at peril with the indigenous community. The second was, word not only does travel on the street but also, like any newsworthy outlet, is able to build mountains from molehills or tear down the most obstinate of structures. And third, you cannot squat within these ranks without an invite. Without any street sense, as they said, I knew that the ranks had opened to allow my entry, even if only a probationary status.

I listened to the hum of conversation about us and wondered how likely it was that if the street people knew about everything, then sooner or later, probably sooner, someone would sell me out for the right price. Perhaps, I figured, it was best to move on while I still had a head start.

While I was yet processing this information, the line began to move forward, Digger engaging various citizens, the denizens of homeless, joking, haggling, and insulting. It was strange to watch the interactions, which appeared to be volatile and yet social. Approximately five feet from the door, an argument of sorts broke out at the back of the line and drew the attention of the doorman. He looked at Digger and said that he'd better look into it before the soup kitchen staff became aware of a problem.

Digger, in reply, said, "Boy, look after my bag and don't let it out of your sights or put it down. Damn tramps be all over it like stink on shit. Meet you inside, and gotta see what these fools are up to."

With that, he stepped out of line, and as he made his way toward the ruckus, he stopped occasionally and drew men, totaling nine in count, from the line. I watched as they approached the quarreling figures. I had the distinct impression that this type of self-policing was well ordered and sanctioned by the hosting community. As the tramp patrols surrounded the men, I saw Digger step between them and speak. I couldn't hear what was being said, nor could I distinguish whom it was said to, but from the distance I observed that one of the would-be combatants was not having any type of peaceful settlement in regards to whatever caused the mysterious issue. As this fellow took on a posturing stance of defiance, in a blink of an eye and in one smooth motion, the congregation of secret police converged on the disrupter, bound him with rope, gagged him to suppress any screaming, and carried him like a sack of potatoes into the alleyway, away from prying eyes. Just like that, a hostile situation was suppressed! The other man stepped back in line and was allowed to take his original spot. Momentarily, Digger emerged from the alley, and while he walked past the line, an occasional pat on the back and complimentary jibes would be called out to him. Though he was in his glory, he never gloated, but with eyes directly on me, he came up to where I stood and I handed him his bag. When our turn came, we went into the feeding hall. Keeping my eyes forward and not looking back, I imitated Digger's moves, attempting at blending in. Needless to say, I stood out like a green thumb on the Pillsbury Doughboy!

When we entered into the feeding ground, a host of aromas assailed my nose, scents of cooking food, musty bodies, last night's lingering odors of a heavy bout of drinking, and hints of recently smoked reefer. Digger headed to the food trays and selected two of the plastic trays, handing me one at the same time, saying, "Boy, it's all soup, carrot soup, bean soup, potato soup, beef stock soup…" And a litany of others, which I had stopped listening for when I saw the buffet-style setup of soups, with servers on the other side.

As if reading my mind, he quickly added that normally he was early enough to be a server and that they got the best before everyone else got there. Of course, being stuck on stupid, I said, "What! The best soup?"

For a moment, he looked at me as if I had just come from another planet, and said, "No, dummy. How in the hell you think they make soup?" Before I could say anything else stupid, he said, "Boy, they get the meats, fruits, cookies, and cakes. 'Course they leave slim pickin's to the rest of us, but that's why I get here early! Damn, boy, you sure you your mama's child? Did she have any that lived?"

At that minute, I had enough with all that "boy" shit, and I'd be damned if I was going to start taking another line of shit, which was going to keep them degrading me! Not to take this insult without a fight, I said, "That's what she told me! Hell, right now you my daddy, so you tell me if she had any kids that lived!"

With that exchange, he stopped, looked at me like I had just smacked him in the mouth. The seconds ticked, with him staring at me and me intently staring back at him in defiance. As sure as the sun in the sky, he busted into a howling gale of laughter, sounding like a hyena, until tears began to run down his cheeks. I was absolutely unprepared for this response, and the scene was so contagious I began to laugh my defensive anger away. He slapped me on the shoulder and said, "Let's find a seat before we got sit on the floor. Damn, that was a good one, boy!" Then he began searching for seats. Just like that, a potentially hostile situation was defused.

I learned something in that instance that I keep with me today. Most of the time, the problems I perceive actually are things that I create. Certain feelings that are not resolved, or perhaps I can't identify what the actual problem is. I become frustrated and take it out on others and various ways. In that moment, I felt like some kind of dunce after Digger had laughed and then invited me in camaraderie to find a seat. Looking at the crowd and accommodations, I didn't really think that the floor wasn't a bad idea, especially as I got a good look at my eating companions and the horrific odors in the room.

As we threaded our way through an assortment of crowded tables, Digger speaking to everyone in the process, he led us to a back table that only had room for five but was crowded with eight chairs. Digger nodded for me to find a seat quickly at the table, which already had four bodies at it. Sitting across from me, he spoke to the already-grazing bodies, and between the loud slurping of soup and open mouth-chewing of bread, I heard him say, "How do, everybody?" He received nods and gestures in acknowledgment from all, except the woman who sat next to me layered in clothing and a hooded sweatshirt. All too soon I would find out to stay out of her way and to respect what she had to say.

Digger, through plastic spoonfuls of soup and sopping bread, said I was the boy that helped ole Shoes out that morning. This won some approving nods from the motley group—that is, all but the woman beside me who had multiple fragrances of unwashed body and decay. Not letting the moment of introduction die, I turned to her and said, "My name is Michael," extending my hand in greeting. Well, what happened next taught me a very valuable lesson. Up until that moment, I had not seen her face, because of the clothing plus the hoodie. When she did raise her head and turned to me, my god, I saw she was missing an eye—the left at that! This gave the impression of someone winking though the depressed, orbless socket. Looking straight into my eyes with her one eye, she said, "Eat shit!" Immediately the table and within-earshot patrons of the soup kitchen burst into gales of laughter, with a smattering of harsh coughs. Digger spewed soup and bread into his bowl, and our table companions, nudging one another, were in tears.

I looked at her as she returned to the task of slurping and gouging her face with bread. Digger interrupted my momentary lost moment with a statement that brought me back to harsh reality. "Boy, stop gawking at her or she might hit you with her bat!"

Looking at him, I turned my eyes back to my attacker without turning my head, and indeed, the small slugger between her legs covered with layers of clothing lay readily available for batting practice. Shaking my head, I wondered how I was going to make this day with these maniacs! Good Lord, up until this day, life on the road had been, for the most part, relatively steady in its monotony. Little did I know at that time I had an education coming.

The rest of the luncheon session went without further incidence, other than occasional dropping of the F-bombs, which I came to understand was the most commonly used verbal phrasing among this underclass.

The announcement was made that we would have to exit the premises. There was widespread grumblings and screeches from the ranks. Additionally, with this announcement people started to dig in their bags for various containers or plastic bags and started stuffing the remainder of bread into them, all the while cussing like drunken sailors and tying shoes. Later, I would learn that after sitting awhile before you start any movement, you were to inspect and readjust your "wheels"—your shoes! The reason is quite simple and very prudent to adhere to: the next move might be the one to save or end your life! The last thing you needed was for your feet not to be working properly.

A roadman's well-being begins with his feet; hence, they are to be cared for and pampered, just as you would a significant other. Your very existence is dependent on mobility.

Gathering the items that he had brought, as well as the newly acquired ones that had been haggled and argued for over lunch exchanges, Digger told me that we must get back to the catch stash before that blasted foreman of the job called to empty the dumpster.

CHAPTER 8

Meeting with the Jew Man

I quickly followed his footsteps, careful not to cause any of the unknown social breaches, and when we arrived back to the site, Digger said, "Boy, we got to make quick work of this if we plan to eat tonight and get a bottle before getting into the mission for the night." Again, I noticed that he used the word *we*; I was included in his plans for securing both a moment of pleasure and that of security. Most of us never give thoughts to the basic rudiments of shelter, security, food, belonging, and the luxury of comfort, but I had learned, or was learning, from the primal ranks of humanity what it meant to be a real social animal.

The town was now in full swing of community life. At lunchtime, people were breaking from jobs to run errands before reporting back to work. School was in recess, and groups of children walked and jostled about. Just like with Shoes, people acknowledged Jigger as though he was a long-standing community member, and he was in his glory, tipping his hat at the ladies and standing tall toward the men. I really couldn't discern what was happening as we traveled back to our trash trove, but I sensed that it was important for survival. Not being able to speak for any other country, I do believe I have the authority to say, "Life on the street, any street, is nothing but a survival game, not advancement to a higher place, but merely a game of not being eaten alive."

The construction crew had started back to work by the time we had arrived. I could hear Digger's undertoned cursing as he reached for the mysteriously refilled grape drink bottle. I looked at him as he shook his head from side to side, and asked, "Digger, what's wrong?"

I did expect some type of tirade, but instead he answered, "Boy, we got a heap of work to do, and we got to do it quick and work around that crew throwing trash in."

I saw his point as we peered over the edge, our catch piles having been covered, and it appeared the crew had worked through lunch. He looked so deflated that I said, "Hey, old man, I got an idea, but you got to tell me what you think about it."

He looked at me with an appraising, surprised look, as if he had seen a flying pig! Before he could respond, I told him that I would climb in the dumpster because I remembered where our main treasures were and he could stay outside and watch out and warn me when the crew would be dumping. Watching him figuring caused me to smile inwardly, because he was actually keen on the idea but was giving the impression that he was still in charge. I told him time was wasting. Pretending that he was reluctant about the idea, he said, "Get to it, boy!" There was that "boy" again; however, this time it didn't hackle my fur. Having figured earlier how to get into the dumpster, I quickly scrambled over the top and made my way to where I thought our catch stash was. A pair of workers' gloves landed beside my feet, and Digger said, "You gonna need these."

Without any hesitation or thought, I put them on and went to work removing the top layer of debris and called out to digger what pile he wanted me to start tossing out to be put in his cart. Occasionally, he'd call out, "Here they come, boy!" and I would climb out on the other side and wait for the workers to finish dumping. As soon as the "All clear!" was sounded, my dumpster diving commenced again. On the outside I would hear every now and then that "Ahhhhhh!" sound, knowing that he was swigging from his bottle, with Digger's coaching and accolades of "Damn, boy, you're better than a tunnel rat!" I didn't know what a tunnel rat was—couldn't be good—but it made me feel good that I was being appreciated and he was pleased. So maybe a tunnel rat isn't a bad thing!

From outside, Digger said we got enough for a few loads and said he'd climb in and look around for more valuable trash, being that I didn't know what to look for in valuable trash. I couldn't argue with that.

As he clambered in, a little unsteady on his feet, he began his hunt. As he hunted about, my mind started to replay the morning. I suddenly remembered the talk about something called a mission while at lunch. I tried to wrap my mind around what a mission might be. My fellow patrons had spoken of it with reverence, and some with disdain. When the thought became too much, I finally was willing to risk the wrath of Digger while still following his instruction of what to do and how to do it. I asked him, "Mr. Digger," hoping the surname would defuse any hostile rebukes, "what's a mission?" This question sent him into a tirade of cuss words and talking to himself in some type of new language! Just when I was thinking that I'd caused him to have a heart attack or stroke, he stopped abruptly and, as calm as you please, explained that the mission was a building that the "Goody Two-shoes" bought to keep the tramps off the street at night. He went on to elaborate that it was just for show and that they were only concerned about themselves and their safety.

Of course, I had an opinion about what he was saying, so without any other thought, I said, "It sounds like they are at least trying to do right." You know, opinions are like buttholes—everyone got one. Most folks can't see their own, so why would you want to look at someone else's? Keep it to yourself! I know that now, but I didn't then; therefore, I was about to have another teachable moment for the umpteenth time today. It was only about two thirty to three in the afternoon. *My god, I'd be dead by nightfall,* I thought, *if it kept going this way!*

He stopped and looked at me for a long moment. I could see and feel the slow boil as I watched his narrow body drunk-sway and his glassy eyes begin to focus. The explosive "What?" Then, "Boy, you stupid! Every time I believe you're going to be okay, you say something that makes me know you just going to die just as dumb as a rock!"

I had had enough! Raising my voice, taking menacing steps toward him, I said, "Old man, I'm going to ask you one more time about this mission shit, and if you don't believe that you can talk about it like you have some sense, then shut the fuck up!"

Again, here we were, standing in this dumpster like two gun-slingers, for the umpteenth time, and he got a glazed look like he was going to pass out, "Hot damn, boy, you got some fire in you!" He laughed and ambled toward me through the debris and, in a calm, uncommonly controlled voice, began to explain something like this: "Son, it's obvious you'd be curious about the hows, whys, and what-nots of why we do what we do, but right now I ain't got the time to explain it to you, because time ain't on our side. But later we can talk. What I'm going to tell you is good information. Boy, it's good information now and will always be good information forever, being that you've chosen the life on the road. There are many ways of learning things. Sometimes we get to learning one basic way, and at others we have to learn a different way. For now, let's just say, to learn this way of life, of course you got to ask questions and prac-tice the ropes of tramping to get it down. However, boy, you got to do more observing than talking. You see, life on the road is about learning, and most learning comes through seeing. That is, no matter how people explain things to you, it all boils down to 'monkey see, monkey do.' Ain't any shorts in that, and never will be. Just be quiet and listen and do. In time you will see what is what. Boy, you got to trust me on this, just like I trusted Shoes when he told me to look out for you. I didn't spend time 'jabberjawing' with him—I just did what he asked. That's trust, and trust don't just come from here." He pointed to his head. "It comes from here," he continued, pointing to his heart. "Now, I said we will talk later. Do you trust what I said?" I nodded that I did. He said, "We got to get to moving. We've wasted good time. I just hope that it was worth it."

He spoke with authority and calmness. I observed that he wasn't swaying from the potent drink that he had been drinking from, and his eyes were clear. As a matter of fact, they were downright piecing as he steadily gazed at me. What I took away from his dialogue were several things. One, this man was intelligent, though a hobo. Second, that he cared about my well-being. And third, he taught me about what loyalty and assumption of responsibility were about. I could not imagine that responsibility and integrity had anything to do with being a nomad. At that moment, what was crystal clear was that I was in the presence of wise men and that, for whatever reason, fate was showing my undeserving behind favor. I actually was beaten down by compassion, which now made me teachable.

We made good time sorting the catch piles and tying rope around copper tubing and aluminum. When all items were ready to his satisfaction, he told me to go climbing from the dumpster. We could see the workers ending their day, and Digger shifted into high gear with instructions that I find items he called out. I was sent to find boxes, plastic to wrap items in, crates, strips of cloth, etc. Returning, I called to him, and he began to hand out our booty. Then, with the last item handed out, Digger leaped from the side, just as nimble as an acrobat, and began organizing the cart. Once everything that could fit in the cart was tied down with yet another rope, he declared that it was break time. I was in agreement because at least an hour and a half had gone by since our dumpster parlay.

Sitting while leaning with his back to the dumpster, he placed his feet up on the cart, produced a bottle of soda from one of his many pockets, and began taking deep, long pulls from it. After several swallows, he offered me to follow in pursuit. I had learned enough not to decline such an offer, because it represented camaraderie. For real for real, I needed a drink! Drinking to quench my thirst, I took in a mouthful. As I swallowed the thick liquid, I knew that this was not grape soda! Great God Almighty, the rancid liquid burned my mouth, throat, and stomach! Directly behind came the numbing, and thereafter the feeling of ease and comfort. Digger watched this process with practiced eyes, and as the feeling of wellness in the universe spread over my body, he said, "Good soda, ain't it, boy?" I had been duped—that had been for sure. The only thing I could do was to agree. Damn good soda indeed!

There were a few moments of silence when he said, "Boy, you got any questions?"

Shaking myself from my reverie and retying my shoelaces, without looking up, I said, "Mr. Digger, where are we going now, and when will I get to see Mr. Shoes again?"

My respectful question and the added "Mr." with formal etiquette floored him. For a moment I didn't think that he'd answer, but after a few long seconds, he said, "I ain't anybody's mister, but thank you anyway. It has been years since anyone said anything that kind to me. Boy, I see why ole Shoes took a shine to you! Matter of fact, I'm beginning to think that you sho 'nuff all right myself. Now, before you open that pie hole and mess everything up, let me let you know where to, how come and when we be meeting Shoes." Digger was like a changed man as he explained that we were going to the scrap man, an old Jew, as he called him, and then meet Hustler. Hustler was said to be able to sell water to fish and ice cubes to Eskimos! He tickled himself into another coughing fit with that line, and I laughed also, just because he tickled me with his outburst of gaiety. We strapped, taped, and juggled our bundles and started toward the direction of the rail yards, where everything had started. A couple of blocks from there, I began to hear barking and braying of dogs. We turned onto a tidy, unpaved dirt road. As I pushed the junk cart and Digger carried several bundles on his shoulder, I noticed how quiet the lane appeared, other than the occasional barks of dogs. We were heading toward the braying hounds. I slowed my pace, ensuring that my small knife was accessible. Then I cautiously followed Digger, though he marched like a queen's guard with authority.

As we got closer to the fence, I was able to see that the property was well maintained. I began to see heaps of assorted metals, old appliances, aluminum, and many items I could not identify. This was organized chaos, with a certain artistic flair. At this time Digger stopped his march and turned to me, saying, "Boy, you do what I tell you: keep quiet, and no matter what, if those dogs come up to you, just let them sniff you and stand still." Without another word, he turned in the direction of the heaps and whistled. It was long, loud, and practiced. Once he had sounded, the dogs, about seven in all, came from all directions. I stepped a few paces from him and watched him cussing the dogs, and the dogs snarling a yapping at him. Inside the grounds, I heard a voice telling the animals to quiet down.

From around a shack building came an older man wearing what appeared to be a beanie. His beard was as white as snow, and he was as thin as a rail yet walked with deliberate steps. He wore a vest and a light-yellow or dingy-white shirt, with the sleeves rolled to the elbow, and brown or black chino pants. His feet were in black brogans, worn but not out. The shoes were well-kept and buffed to a dull sheen. He approached the rails of the fence. The animals had quieted down, except for a small mongrel that continued to snort short yaps, until the master placed his hands on its head and said, "You have done good. Now be quiet." He said it in a hush-toned baritone voice. With that, all was quiet. When he raised his head, he looked at Digger, through round steel-rimmed glasses, and then at me. I was standing back; his searching eyes were gray and piercing, but they were kind. Even from the distance of about ten feet, I identified within them a depth of understanding wisdom that only came as a result of a lifetime of experience. I immediately liked this unknown person and the relationship that had developed between him and my fast-becoming tribe. This was unexplainable then, and today, as I think back on this incidence, it is still unexplainable. I felt no threat or condemnation in his presence.

Having seen me observing him, he turned his attention back to Digger and, in a compassionate yet business voice, said, "Mr. Digger, I see that you've brought some items for exchange. You and your associate please meet me at the exchange area, if you will. I'll meet you in a few moments." He turned, and the dogs followed him in an orderly fashion along the fence line. Digger waited until he was out of earshot and told me to gather the things from certain bundles and to leave the rest and follow him.

The voice of this Jew man was calm, baritone, and measured. All the while that I followed Digger, he spoke in hush-toned whispers of the things yet to be done prior to meeting with Shoes. However, as I followed obediently, I really was missing most of what he was saying, because I thought of this Jew man and actually what part he played in the lives of this brood of nomads and why it appeared that he was an honorable man of distinction and yet one that actually cared for the downtrodden. How I came to this or these conclusions is beyond me, but I still believe it true today. There indeed are some unexplainable truths, which words or minds will never understand. Proceeding along the outside property line, I saw that the heaps of debris were actually orderly separations of various wirings, metals, and bits and pieces of materials of solid masses.

Arriving at a gate, Digger turned and said to me to remain quiet and speak when spoken to. Knowing that I had further questions, he added, "Boy, there are strange workings going on in life. This is just one of them—we'll talk later. Okay?" With that we stood and waited for the return of the Jew. There are moments that even if others don't mention, you can tell when you're experiencing an other-than-normal common thing. This was definitely one of those moments now! So yes, my eyes would stay open, and my mouth clammed.

Shortly, he came around a small standing shed carrying a small tray, and on it I saw four sandwiches and four cans of soda. The sandwiches were wrapped in aluminum foil; these he set on an upended bucket and stepped to the gate and lifted the latch to the gate and bade us to enter. Seeing my hesitation to enter, he assured me that the dogs had been put away and would not bother the invited guests. Truth be told, the dogs and their behavior were more normal of the two. Being in his presence was both unsettling and comforting. The dogs had primal understanding, but he was beyond my scope.

Following Digger's direction and small comments from the Jew man about the placement of items, all our treasure was now on sight, inventoried. I stepped back and found a bucket to sit on to watch this ritual transaction begin. I had a feeling that I was at a gladiator type of bout as the two combatants entered the arena, beginning to feel one another out with dodges and parries. In all of this, there was no noise from the brood of dogs, which were not seen. It was as though we had been transported to a place of calm. Prior to their bartering engagement, the Jew man turned to me and said, "Rest a spell, eat, and drink," while he and Digger began their business. How he said this was more of an instruction than an invite; I was dismissed, albeit with courtesy and flair, but none the less told that I had nothing to say about anything. This suited me just fine; I was exhausted from trying to interpret and process and keep pace with everything that had started since sunrise until now. My head still swam with memories and new information.

Selecting one of the sandwiches, popping the lid on the soda, I started with a small sip and was just as happy as a kid in a candy store, not being part of anything at that moment.

What appeared to be hours in duration bartering were nothing but about twenty minutes of bantering, in which Digger and the Jew man exchanged comments about quality, rarity, density, and worth. Occasionally I'd hear Digger exclaim, "Damn, you're killing me here! Come on, you can do better than that!" Or "Man, you got to be shitting me!" At one round of the negotiations I heard Digger tell the Jew, "I was born at night, but not last night!" Sometimes you'd hear the Jew man say, "Mr. Digger, be reasonable." Of course, following that plea, you'd hear Digger say, "Reasonable? Reasonable! If I let you get it for that, I won't have an ass to be reasonable with!"

Watching the hustle going on before me, listening to the leaves rustling in the trees and the occasional swat at the winged insects, I was lulled into a dream state of semisleep, the sun just warm enough and not too hot, I sat and lightly slumbered. Dream-thinking of my days prior to this morning in the rail yard, I stood in the window, concealed by a ragged curtain, peering out, watching my mother as she smoked in front of the homestead. I knew she was watching for me. "I'm sorry," I said. "I'm sorry." Just as the grief began to mount, I was being shaken from the surreal haze and rushed into the conscious reality. I remembered that I didn't want to continue reliving the hurtful memory again. However, over the years it would become a scene of a replaying tape quite often.

"Okay, boy, this job is finished. Time we be going!" Digger looked just like the cat that swallowed the canary—he beamed from ear to ear! No one needed to tell me that he'd swapped the items we had brought for a good price! Though I remembered the Jew's eyes, the depth and the wisdom that I'd seen in them, I kind of figured perhaps Digger had indeed duped him once or twice in the negotiations, or at least thought that he had.

As we gathered the items that were discarded and not used in the barter session, the Jew man stood by, sorting through his recent purchases. I would see him closely inspect then place the item in an appropriate pile. He was steady and methodical. After a while, he turned to Digger and asked if he might speak to me privately for a moment. I thought this was strange, to ask permission to speak to me while I was right there; he could have asked me! What I didn't know then that I do now is that this was a form of respect of person and ranking within the pecking order. Obviously, Digger had approved, because a voice came into my ear. "May I have a word with you, young man?" Turning toward him and simultaneously looking at Digger, who nodded his approval before replying that he didn't mind, I saw the Jew man turn, motioning for me to follow.

I slowly followed the Jew man toward a well-worn path leading to the shed entrance. I noticed that his property was well maintained and he had chosen landscaping that was both sparse and functional. While we walked, several of the dogs that we encountered walked and sniffed about the area, but none seemed to pay any attention to me or the owner. Once in the entry of the shed, the Jew man turned and looked back at the yard, at the sky, and paused and looked at me while motioning for me to come up the three steps and join him inside. I knew that any discussion that we were to have had nothing to do with the bartering and haggling of junk.

Ascending the three steps, the man had already entered the small space and had his back to me. And when I entered the structure, I was amazed by how small yet spacious it appeared. It was orderly and furnished with a dark wood table and three sturdy chairs that were very plain. Along the back wall ran a workbench with a barstool type of chair and various woodworking tools hung orderly on a peg board hanger. I spied at the end of the bench a small coffeepot sitting on a small propane hot plate, steam rising from it.

With his back still to me, he began by explaining the disparity of the haves and the have-nots within our society. It felt that he watched me though turned from me. I just knew that he understood that I was absorbing the moment, and he waited patiently as I moved from one assessment to another, and then he'd place another puzzle piece into the frame of understanding. He elaborated on how, at certain times in life, conditions and circumstances cause individuals to make choices and actions that place them into situations that are actually designed by what is called fate. All through his discourse, he worked deliberately to rearrange tools, small pieces of various metals, on the countertop and drawers at his workbench, and removing two cups from the wall pegs, he poured the hot water from the pot. His voice had the timbre of a teacher's and the patient cadence of a loving parent's. Finally, he turned to face me and asked that I seat myself in one of the folding chairs beside his desk. So captivated by the room and its atmosphere of calm and the timbre of his voice, I didn't take notice of the rolltop desk that sat in the corner underneath a small-paned window overlooking the backyard. Taking the warm cup of water, I went to the chair next to the desk to await my host. He came carrying a small tin and his cup. When he sat down, he was silent, arranging the tin and cup on the desk. As he opened it, I saw a small metal scooper and what appeared to be tea leaves of some type. He scooped a careful measuring and dumped the contents into my cup. I watched as the hot water browned with color and the leaves began to saturate with water and submerge to the bottom. He methodically did the same to his and placed the scoop and lid within the tin and set it aside. Never once was the silence uncomfortable, and during the ritual of making the drinks, I was compelled to remain silent as well. It all seemed just the right thing to do, and anything else would have sullied the moment.

When I saw my host pick up his cup and gently blow on it, sipping after, I followed suit in practiced imitation. For a few quiet moments, we did not speak or watch each other; instead, we enjoyed the quietude and breathed. After the right space of time, my host, still holding his cup, turned and pierced me with his wizened gaze. He stated, "Now, let me give you information, and what you do with it is your choice. Always remember, young sir, information is nothing but just that. In itself, information is neutral. Giving it value, whether it is positive or negative, totally rests on the perception of the receiver and what chosen actions are followed. There will always be consequences for these actions. Consequences, just like information, are again a neutral occurrence. We call it sometimes the law of cause and effect. Dear boy, what I am saying is that no matter how anyone paraphrases any of this, it comes down to this: our choices make our destiny. Therefore, what I am about to tell you may or may not be understood. However, it is applicable to you."

Up until this point of the conversation, even if you could call it that, the Jew man had not asked my name. And now he did. I replied, "Michael." He leaned back in his chair and removed his wire-framed glasses, staring into the backyard. While nibbling at one of the glasses' arms, with a distant look in his eyes, slowly he nodded, as if an affirmation had been revealed to him. Slowly, too, he turned his head to me, and I could see the full measure of his face, but his eyes were the focus. The gray of the eyes, the intensity, the weight, the searching, not for conviction or absolution, but that of begging to be understood. Now, this was not the type of understanding for which I needed to understand him, but for me to understand this information was only for me!

"Did you know that there is an archangel named Michael?" he asked. I nodded that I did. Slowly but deliberately he began, "It is said that when Michael is called to war for the Almighty, he does so with tears in his eyes. It is the compassion and love that he has for the enemy that causes him sorrow, as he becomes the judgment of God executed. This says much to the nature of our Creator, for though mankind rallies against his holiness, he yet loves us. Even in the times in which he exerted the death of multitudes, he did so in pain and sorrow. This is why we see that throughout the lineage of history, he has forgiven and redeemed even the worst of our sins. More so, to send his Son as the blood sacrifice? Oh my, what love!"

Until that moment of dialogue, I had never given any more thought to God and punishment. I figured he got pissed and did what he had to do to show man who was really running the show. Of course, I accepted the fact that he forgave, but I didn't, until that moment, consider what price he paid in his heart to censure or destroy any part of his creation. However, having truly heard the Jew man's interpretation pricked a spot within me that rang true.

Gathering himself from the reveries of his internal thoughts, he crossed his legs and replaced the glasses onto his face. "Michael, exactly where you've come from and where you are going and, most importantly, why you are here now, all this means something. Instead of spinning our proverbial wheels, trying to figure out the plans of God, I think it more prudent to pay attention to the present moment, because the present always dictates the future."

That made sense to me. Yet I was still wondering why we were having a conversation in the first place.

As if reading my mind, he smiled and said, "You may be wondering why we are talking. You don't know me, nor I you." Without waiting for any acknowledgment from me, he continued. "Along this path that you have chosen to walk, there are many unexplainable circumstances. Lives on the roadways are like none other. The vistas that you see will be large, and yet in the panoramic viewing, you will see the true smallness of things." At that moment, I must have looked either confused or just downright dumb—no matter which—because he shook his head and said, "Never mind all that for now. Later it will all become clear for you."

"Little brother," he continued, "word travels fast in this small community. You are being revered as a savior and protector. I understand that this is not what you expected or wanted, and believe me, I know that sometimes life does things that just don't fit in with our personal plans." With that statement, he smiled, or at least just the hint of a smile, which allowed me to see youthfulness hidden just beneath the old skin. "Son, I do not know if you consider spiritual things or not, and for the most part, it doesn't matter whether you do or not. What is important is that I will tell you some things that are important, and perhaps in time you'll remember what is being said today and maybe it will make a difference in where you'll be and where you wish to go."

I sat across from him, and my mind went to a distant past, in one of which I sat across from my Master as he explained the reason that sometimes a man must simply disappear. Although my mind was swimming in the memory of the day with my Master, the final day, I was altogether present in the here and now with the Jew.

"It is not by chance that you are here. I can see you are not from the same ilk as the people that you are now involved with. For whatever reason or circumstance, God has brought you here for a reason and his purpose. One day it will be revealed. Michael, we are not to waste our time trying to figure the revelation. A revelation must become revealed after the constructs of experiences have been participated and lived throughout. You may not understand this at this time, but trust me, in time all the information that you gather during your journey in life will come together and give you a realization. At the time of this realization, or some call it an epiphany, there will be choices to be made and an action or actions to be performed. Entirely dependent on the time, location, and desired outcome. And you and you alone will be responsible for all scene placement and production and, yes, even destruction. There is one thing to keep presence of mind about, and that is that each of us that is given life into this world is placed here by design. Having said this, know that there will be times in which you'll not be able to consult another on which course of action you should choose. At those moments, you must rely heavily upon the things that you alone have learned. This is the destiny of all mankind. As for the present, I can tell you this: School is now in for you. The things that you are about to learn are for the future, and so therefore we know you will pass through this period. The Master gave you certain endowments with skills and knowledge to help others. And now your path has begun."

I sat and listened to his baritone voice, and my mind raced and feelings rippled within me, some of which I could identify, and others unknown. The things that he spoke of and the sincerity of his voice blockaded any tendrils of doubt in what he said was nothing but true.

A shrilling whistle danced about the air. He looked toward the backyard through the small sash, smiled, and said, "It appears that Mr. Digger has sounded the bell to end this class. If you take nothing else from this conversation today, it is important to remember this: no matter what befalls you from this time forth, always know that you will live! No matter what, you will live!"

Those final fatal words should have caused me to start sweating bullets; however, the effect was, a calming and a sense of serenity shrouded me. Unable to speak momentarily, I nodded that I understood, even though all this was beyond me. He stood, and I followed him toward the door as Digger's squeaky voice replaced the serious baritone sound with, "Dammit, Jew Man, we got to get to rolling! You know we got to get that boy to a safe place tonight because those Clay boys don't like it much that they got the short end."

The Jew man stepped onto the porch, and I weaved my way from behind in time to see and hear the hounds had reacted to the whistle and were giving ole Digger the canine dickens by barking and jumping up the wooden plank boards. All the while Digger was yelling, "Get! Get!" Just like on our arrival, the master called the dogs by name and told them to be quiet. Then there was silence; the only thing to be heard was mumbling from Digger outside the fence. As I passed the Jew, he reached out and touched my shoulder, saying, "Remember what I have said." Nodding in acknowledgment, I descended the stairs and headed toward the fence.

Digger had been so preoccupied with the braying hounds he had not seen our exit from the small shed. As I came nearer to the fence line, he stopped cussing the dogs and called out, "Boy, we got to get moving, and I mean *now*!"

I spoke up, saying, "Okay." That startled him, because I was so near and he hadn't seen me because of his dog watching.

"Shit," he said, "you got to quit sneaking up on people, boy!" I only smiled and said, "Yes, sir."

Digger hollered at the man on the porch and said, "Shoes's gonna have my left nut if we don't get!"

The Jew man responded, "Tell Mr. Shoes that I was the delay. I needed to speak to the young man."

With the exchange complete, Digger said, "Let's get to movin', 'cause time ain't on our side." He had haggled most of our treasure, and some still remained in the cart, but at least the bundles were gone.

CHAPTER 9 ———————————

Unofficially Adopted

I had to push the cart as we headed off to God knows where at breakneck pace. All the while, with the only interruptions being from "Turn here," "Turn there," "Wait a minute," and "Hell, hurry up," my mind still echoed with the fateful words "You will live."

At present, I am unable to recall exactly what we did with the remaining stash or, for that matter, exactly how we wound up at the feeding ground where we were to meet Shoes. My mind and consciousness were still in the small shed. It wasn't so much as remembering with my mind, but the best that I can recall is the nuance of emotions and stirring feelings that were at play within me. Sometimes my mind would take the lead and I'd try to recall word for word what the strange Jew man had said. Try as I may, I always conclude to the very last words: "You will live."

Coming out of whatever state one would call it, I became aware that now I was listening to the constant chatter of Digger, most of it to himself, and at other times to me, and the shout-outs to passing pedestrians and hand waves across streets that we passed. The workday was drawing to a close, and school had recessed. You know each place, though different in many respects, still holds to some same standards. Each place sleeps, then comes to life and then recesses for a while, and then sleeps again, only to awaken the next day. Some say it's the same old, same old, but I have learned that that concept is very wrong. I have learned that each day brings with it, yes, the remnants of yesterday, but an adventure in living that can never be repeated. That's the secret of truly living. Being in the day, each second of each moment, each hour, and the accumulation of minute experiences that fulfill the day, never to be seen again. That sounds pretty deep; it may be, but it took years for that to come to me.

As we walked, I became aware I no longer had the shopping cart. To this day, I just don't remember what we did with it. The only thing that I know for certain is that I began to see more of the disenfranchised (homeless) people in neighborhood that we walked. The buildings began to appear to be older, I dare say, ancient monoliths. I'm not saying that this part of town was seedy; however, the sheen was not as lustrous, yet it did remain quaint, as was the rest of the town, in description.

We finally arrived at a building that seemed to be an old church with a reconstructed addition to it. I could see the large neon sign made in the emblem of the holy cross, which read, "Jesus Saves." People of different colors, sexes, and builds stood in a semiorderly line, and there were some groups that clustered together, talking with one another. As I was slowing my pace, Digger called, "Keep up, boy!" Quickening to catch up with him, I ogled this place and the people. "There's Shoes. You stand right here and hold my bag while I go gab with him." Taking his bag, I decided to sit on the small stone wall that ran the length of the sidewalk along the building. I could keep my eye on him and Shoes and, at the same time, continue to people-watch without being too obvious. Digger crossed the street to approach Shoes, who was talking to the woman that had told me to eat shit earlier at the noon meal, and two other men. They all greeted Digger as though he was a long-lost friend. I scanned the area with interest. Though this was the downside of what I had seen of the town earlier, the surrounding wasn't bad. A small park was adjacent to this place across the street, and looking down the road a ways, I could see several churches. Standing and taking Digger's bag with me, I started to walk the length of the building to better identify what it was. Coming to the front, I could see a sign that said, "City Mission." So now I knew what a mission truly was.

Upon discovering what this gathering place was, I had satisfied my minimal curiosity and started back to the spot that I had been told to wait in. Arriving back to the original general area, I found that my spot had been taken by two elderly gents quietly speaking to each other. Several tramp bags were lying on the sidewalk. Ignoring the bags, I stood behind the two men.

I could still see Shoes, Digger, the cussing lady, and others animatedly talking and could hear the occasional laughter. Sometimes, when things slow down, your mind begins to travel on its own accord. That was exactly what started with me; I was lulled by the murmuring of multiple conversations, the quiet of the day, and the activity of doing nothing but waiting in line. It really didn't occur to me what I was waiting for, but I was content just the same.

I had only been on the road for a few months. I had basically traveled alone and kept to myself. Every once in a while, a road companion would travel a couple of days together, only because our destinations paralleled or intersected for a period. I had slept in doorways, loading docks, abandoned cars, or buildings. Many nights I slept outside under the stars, being eaten alive by the night insects.

There had been times I had been run off from some doorways or harassed by the police for sleeping in parks or other unsavory spots. One time I thought I'd found a temporary oasis near a pasture that had apple, pear, and cherry trees. Climbing the apple tree was easiest because it was the youngest; I gathered several and decided perhaps a couple of pears would be fine after a meal of potted meat and a drink from a small meandering brook. I set my apples at the base of the tree because I would need all my monkey limbs to get up the trunk to the nearest low-hanging branch. After a couple of futile attempts, I started my Spiderman impersonation. I sensed more than heard something, and while clinging to the trunk, I turned my head and was almost eyeball-to-eyeball with a big black bull. I can't adequately describe the snorting and huffing sound it made, but I can say it was none too pleased with me clinging to what I now surmised to be its tree and pasture. Suddenly seeing it, and it seeing me, the bull charged. No longer thinking about apples or pears, in shock, I had loosened my grip just for an instance. I bear-hugged as much of the tree as I could for purchase and started to gorilla-climb. Up I went, but not before I could hear, "Mooooo!" then felt and heard a *thunk*, and then feeling the vibration as the beast rammed the trunk again! I scrambled up that tree with the practiced ease of a lumberjack after that!

Making it to a sturdy limb, I looked down at it. The bull had the nerve to be looking up at me. Huffing and stomping its hooves and circling the tree. This being my first experience with any real wildlife, this really took some bravado out of my sails. Below was a real monster, and there I sat on a tree, in somebody's field, and a big black bull was waiting for my Black ass. Just when I thought it couldn't get any worse, he circled a couple of times, rubbing himself in the tree bark, then, as pretty as you please, the fucker sat down! At that point it became evident that animals have good sense, because this nonverbally said, "I don't have no place go anytime soon. I'll just wait for you." The only thought to come to me was, *Really!*

After sitting there awhile, I began to get over my fear and started to develop a plan. First, I decided to dive-bomb him with pears. Well, the problem was twofold: one, I wasn't an experienced climber, and two, the limb that I was stuck on didn't have any more than a dozen pear bombs. To get more, I'd have to go up. I didn't relish that idea because I firmly believe what goes up must come down. I put my plan into test. I gathered several and tucked them in my shirt and positioned myself, taking aim. I put just a touch of strength to cause what would be a sting, not hurt it. Bombs away, I hit it on its thick neck! The bull's response was to reach its neck out and nibble at the tossed fruit. The second bomb missed him entirely, and its response was to look upward, as if saying, "I don't have to be anywhere anytime soon, again!" My last dive-bomb hit him on his rump; this didn't even elicit a batting of an ear! Realizing that I was really up the creek, I came up with the idea that I thought was novel: if could piss on him, the human smell would drive him from the tree. I can't tell you where this thought originated, but here it was, and more importantly, there I was, on a tree!

So guess what? Precariously angling myself among the branch and the center of the tree, I whipped it out and let it rip. Several things happened at once. My waterworks was down to a dribble because I was dehydrated. Life on the road causes that frequently. Second, because of me trying to balance and my being dehydrated, I got more piss on me than the bull. The straw that broke the camel's back, however, was when the bull stood and shit on my stash of apples! Pecker in hand, pants wet, I watched as he stood shaking his mighty neck, crapped on my apples, and ambled off as if it were all in a day's work. Long after the bull had left and I watched it cross the field into the tree line, I stayed in the tree. This is the rational reason I didn't come down quickly: If a large bull can sneak up on you while you are climbing a tree, holds you hostage up a tree for a few hours, takes pear bombings and not be bothered, it shows that it's not bothered by you trying to piss on it and shits on your apples—before leaving! Don't you perhaps believe it's smart enough to lie in wait to ambush you! Well, at that time I thought so and decided to stay treed until I could see it might just lose interest with a nigger in a tree. There are some unexplainable truths. Indeed, sometimes fact is stranger than fiction!

Abruptly, I was awakened from this distant memory with a challenging, "Nigga, what you doing in my spot?" I had been leaning on the stone wall behind the two old men when two tramps about my age and size interrupted my dreaming. I was taken aback by the hostility that permeated from both. Each seemed ready to fight, as they chillingly stared. I told them that they were up front but had walked out of line to see the front, and when I returned, others had filled in, so I came to the back and stood behind the old guys. Of course, this appeared to inflame them the more, when one pointed to the bags lying on the sidewalk and said, "Those are ours!" As I looked at the bags, then I knew I had just learned another valuable lesson. This had to do with street reservations for holding spots. I apologized, saying, "I am sorry, I'll just get behind you." However, this did not appease them, because one said, "Naw, nigga, you're going all the way to the back of the line, because other people had been waiting." The others in line had taken notice because of their loud talking and, as I watched, I noticed that most of the onlookers didn't appear to really appreciate these obnoxious two any more than I was beginning to dislike them. What defused the situation was a familiar voice asking if there a was problem. It was Shoes; alongside him were Digger, the cussing lady, and about four more members I didn't recognize. The two ruffians answered together, that wasn't anything happening, and with that answer, Shoes and party just stepped in front of them as though they had already been in line all along. Digger came to me and said, "Damn, boy, can't leave you alone for a minute! Shit!"

Someone from inside of the building came out. They were walking and counting people in the line. I asked Shoes what was going on. He answered, "They only have a certain number of beds, and the rest have to get turned away. Anyone that doesn't make it tonight can come back tomorrow. They'll just have to rough it for tonight. You can only get in every other day." Now I could see that meandering line had grown around the block. Throughout the course of the day, I could not have imagined the large number of homeless in this small quaint town, but before my eyes the truth was being told.

Directly behind me, I heard Digger say, "Hey, hustle man, were you able to get to the, Pecker checker?" I didn't really hear anything beyond that, because "pecker checker" stuck out too loudly. I asked, "What's a *pecker checker*?" My compatriots chuckled and downright laughed at my inquiry, and somehow I knew in the fiber of my being that I would soon find out, to their delight. The line of bodies began a slow movement. Shoes stepped beside me and said, "Boy, we're at the mission. We're going to the church meeting first, eat, shower and bed. Before we ate, we got to eat the Word of God. Before we ate food, we showered. After we ate, we slept. Now, stick close and follow my lead."

I nodded as we passed the halfway mark to entering the building.

73

CHAPTER 10

Religion, Food, Shower, Bed

I could hear a piano and some people singing. There were several men in sports jackets and collared shirts passing leaflets out in line and asking if anyone wanted prayer. Digger nudged me in the back with his finger and said, "Boy, you're going to get some old-time religion now!" When we entered the front door, it led to a hallway covered with a worn red carpet that led to a large room with a lot of wooden chairs. In front was a raised dais, which had a heavy wooden podium on it, with a very large thick Bible atop it. Directly above this, a large crucifix hung suspended from the ceiling, with Jesus on it.

I'm guessing approximately seventy-five to one hundred of us were in this tomblike structure. What amazed me was that all of us demonstrated a reverence for such a place and remained quiet and orderly, except for an occasional cough or whispered chuckle. The worship leader was a small chubby specimen of a man who appeared to have spent time in the street life but had been redeemed or reformed. On the small outfitted stage sat a small boom box. He turned it on, and the tape began to play an old spiritual about God troubling water. After the song had played and set the holy atmosphere, he opened with a word of prayer that droned from the beginnings of heaven and earth and continued with the fall of Satan, the birth and death of the Christ, and the world history of sin. My goodness, this ritual prayer covered A to Z of the travails of life and the damnation of all souls!

As the small apostle droned, I began to relax, and the day's travels began to let me know just how tired I was. Shoes nudged me as I began to slip into a light dozing. Gathering my wits, I looked around our motley crowd of members, seeing some dozing, others in rapt attention, and others digging through their belongings.

After this presidential prayer came "Amen," and it resounded from the audience with gusto as well. Then the little man asked if any had a selection that they wished us all to sing. Out of the crowd came, "Let's sing the wretch song!"

I have to pause here and give some information. I believe it important, or at least it became important for me. In all my travels throughout the streets of America, in every single type of mission, outreach, urban ministry, or an out-and-out homeless tent revival, that "wretch like me" song is sang. Many times the congregation doesn't know all the words, but when the refrain comes to the part that says, "Saves a wretch like me," to be sung, almost in every instance all join in and burst forth in song!

Yes, of course, I am talking about the old spiritual "Amazing Grace." I found that this was like the national anthem to the downtrodden masses, and just for us to come together in the unity of this song joined our spirits, and our single plights became a unity moment. We were a nation of wretches saved by grace, even if only for a moment in time. Since my first introduction to this anthem under those circumstances, I have never referred to the song "Amazing Grace" as anything but, and to this day, for me it is the "wretch song."

After the resounding chorus of the wretch song and the lingering hacking coughs, we sat and listened to the slipshod sermon and patiently waited for the altar call to be saved, where about half the audience went forward to accept Jesus as our Savior. Being redeemed had its advantages, I found out. Many attended the call so that they could be on the kitchen duty the next day, which ensured that beds could be held and they would be able to select from the first fruits of breakfast before the multitude of the hungry. Of course, Digger and Hustle Man were two of the first to the altar of salvation to accept Jesus and reserve bed and kitchen duty! All the while Shoes sat stoically beside me and clued me to remain silent and stay in my seat. It wasn't until later that I'd find out what was really happening. However, I can tell you this: it was a marvel to be witnessed through innocent eyes, and the awe still amazes me today, though my eyes have been trained to observe the dynamics of it all. Truly we are wretched, but that doesn't only apply to those of us who have been ostracized, minimized, and disenfranchised by mainstream society.

With the newly redeemed saints returning to their seats, the leader began the benediction for dismissal. Another man, who was big, Black, and somewhat reminded me of a gorilla, came to the podium. He began to speak to quiet the crowd. Shoes leaned over to Digger and said, "Were we able to get everything in order with the pecker checker?"

Digger replied, "Yeah, all set."

With a nod, Shoes fell silent.

I know I shouldn't have said anything, but "pecker checker"? Being between Shoes and Digger, I asked, "Mr. Digger, what's the *pecker checker?*"

"Boy, ya about to find out." With that, he started gagging to contain his laughter, and Shoes just shook his head like, "I just can't take it no more." I miserably sat between them both, resigned to my immediate future fate.

We were herded, row by row, toward a large dining hall and lined up single file to the serving line. Having experienced the after-noon chow down, I was familiar with the jostling of bodies, the smell, and the noise. Trays were at the incoming serving area; you took one, then walked the line with tray in hand and received what was being given out. Tonight, for example, a bowl of soup was handed to you from the server. Moving to the next, you were given a prepared plate with a lump of overcooked rice with gravy, a baked potato, and green beans. As you moved down, an unidentifiable piece of meat was placed on the plate, and you continued with bread and a piece of cake. At the very end of the serving treadmill, a cooler with an attendant gave you watered-downed ice tea. I followed my leaders, Shoes and Digger, as they made their way near the rear of the feeding room and sat at one of the empty tables, which were fast filling up. Strange enough, there sat a large bowl of cut bread in the center of the table. Shoes noticed that I noticed, and before I could comment, he sat and said, "You will find that the name of Bread Lines is for real, boy. Bread is a staple for road life!" We then ate in silence and in the cacophony of the sounds of unwashed bodies and the seas of distant dreams and lives dissolved in the past.

While I concentrated not to think of the mash before me, I sparingly looked at the crowd. Slowly it dawned on me what was missing: I noticed that there were no women and children, while at lunch I had seen that one-third of the lunchroom was made up of women and children of various ages. I suspected that at that time I had not even registered this information on a conscious level. Yet now it was starkly noticeable. I leaned toward Shoes and asked, "Where are the women and children that I saw today?"

"When it comes to the homeless, they separate us, especially at night, so that we don't reproduce."

As the words fell from his lips to my ears, I stopped my panning of the crowd and looked at my food, which I had been trying to eat out of necessity. I vividly remember that moment, and to this day, I cannot ignore the deep sear of sadness and shame that washed over me. While I was yet in this state of being, Shoes continued in a soft, controlled voice, "Son, our particular population is a slap in the face of social humanity. It completely mirrors the wrongs that we do to ourselves and to others. Each day that the regular world comes into contact with one of ours, they are confronted by their own lies and betrayal of being their brother's keeper. We are the stark reality that stands beyond any lie that they can hide behind. We are the truth, in flesh and blood, that equality and equity do not exist. So no matter what any preacher says about how we are forgiven, we must walk in the borderlands and shadows of the world. When the ranks of humanity come into contact with one of ours, there are only two things that stir them: One, pity for us and shame on themselves. The second is anger directed toward us, and shame on them." I truly listened to what he was saying, but when he spoke those last words, I started to ask a question for clarity of the statement. However, this wise man knew my look, and before the words even formed in my throat, he continued to answer an unasked question. "In the first, which is pity in what they see before them, they feel, even though they don't recognize it for what it is. They reach into their pursers and pockets to buy away their guilt. When the second instance comes, this is where they become angry. Again, they don't know why, but I'll tell you. They are angry because we are the reminder of their greed and dishonesty. We are, in essence, them. If circumstances were different, it could be them that would be standing before us for a handout! It doesn't matter whether you're White, Black, Indian, Mexican, or whatever. This contempt is all over the world, and from what I can understand, it's been like this since people began to build what they call social order. All this is nothing but another form of rulership, not leadership."

I'm not saying that I bought all that he was laying down at that time, but as I reflected on my journey thus far, I realized Shoes was not too far off the mark, or let's just say I could not find a plausible counter point of view.

While I thought on these things and tried very hard not to see what was sinking into the warm weak, unsweetened tea, suddenly Hustle Man bumped me from behind. As he leaned between Shoes and me, his odor made our eyes water and us hold our breath, but I was able to hear, "Is all arranged. Make sure the boy is between you and Digger here when we get to the showers." He had said this in an urgent whisper and was again dashing through the feeding hall. Showers? How could anyone smell like that and speak of showers?

For the most part, the rest of the meal was uneventful as we force-fed our faces just to fill our bellies. The lights began to flicker on and off rhythmically, and the hall began to quiet. The big Black man, who reminded me so much of an ape, stood in front of the serving line. All attention was diverted to him. "All right, boys, it's shower time! You know the routine. We don't want any problems tonight, or you will be put out! Anybody caught with any liquor, dope, or weapons will be put out! Anyone caught playing with their pee-pee will be put out. Anybody caught playing with anybody else's pee-pee will be put out!" This last comment caused a rowdy period of laughter, and a few men's names were called out, and they were asked if they understood. Lastly, he said, "If there is any fighting, not only would you be put out, but I'll also kick your ass first! Now, is all that understood?" The response from the crowd was not as enthusiastic, but the general consensus was that it was understood. We were told to keep our seats, and we would be removed one table at a time.

Digger said, "Boy, that be the pecker checker. You stay between me and Shoes when we line up. Don't be wandering off, and don't let nobody in front of you. And for Christ's sake, don't be daydreaming! Dammit, pay attention! Me and Shoes got this."

"Okay, Mr. Digger," I said.

As the tables were being called and moved, I watched the hallway fill with bodies slowly moving to an unknown destination. Our table was called then, and I witnessed firsthand the intense jostling and penning of bodies against one another. I followed Digger's instruction to the letter, and in some instances, I bullied would-be line jumpers with quiet aggression, with solar plexus punches, head-butts, and groin slams. None of these maneuvers drew any attention because of the steady pace of line movement.

I must take a moment to describe how this system was set up. Actually, it was really efficient, though the more compassionate would have considered it a little inhumane. Once individuals entered the corridor from the dining hall, the line meandered at a stop-and-go interval. Turning a corner, one began to see the reason for this. Beyond the line of unwashed bodies, it could clearly be seen that at the end of this narrow corroder, it continued through an arching doorway, minus doors, into a small enclave that widened to twice the size of the hall that we were in. Two men were positioned at the archway on either side of the line. Looking closely, I saw dark-colored bins, I knew they were plastic, because as the men removed one to hand to a person in the line, I could hear the hollow thudding that plastic makes. Coming closer to the enclave, I was able to see the massive pecker checker in chest waders and what appeared to be a rubber-bibbed apron! He was looking periodically toward a doorway, but what was most alarming was the fact that five naked men stood in line as he inspected their bodies before sending each one by one through the doorway, him continuing to watch.

Well, there are times such as this one when it's time to get some answers quickly!

I leaned into Shoes, who was in front of me, and said, "Okay, it's about time to let the cat out of the bag, ole man."

He snickered, not to laugh at my dismay, but to let me know it was all right, just standard operating procedure. "Before anyone gets a bed, they must have a shower. Pecker Checker there ensures that no contraband is sneaked into the mission. His other duty is to make sure everybody at least gets wet, preferably clean. There's always five men butt-ball naked before him so he can see that there are no violations hidden. So you got to lift your balls and show him your ass. You strip when you become the fifth man, your clothes go into a bin, and you are given a number. Don't lose it, because it'll be a MOFO in the morning, because you'll have to wait until all the numbers are returned before you get yo stuff."

That only explained getting in, the pecker check, and the butthole lookee naked, but it didn't say anything about what was on the other side. Was it a nudist mission?

"What do we wear while inside?" I asked hurriedly because we were getting close to the examining part! He said that they had old hospital scrubs that they gave that one had to return before getting one's belongings.

Fifth in line, I was handed a bin and stripped and placed all my stuff in it, got my number, and waited my turn to have my pecker checked. Shoes was before me, and when his turn came, he raised his arms at his sides and slowly turned 360 degrees in front of the ape, turning to spread his ass cheeks after. With a nod from the apelike creature, Shoes stepped through the unknown doorway from sight. I stepped forward, face-to-face with a human that gave some credence to man coming from apes. I imitated what I had seen Shoes do. His deep-set eyes, which were foreshadowed by an overhanging forehead, made it impossible to read what was on his mind. I refused to break eye contact with the beast. He diverted his eyes from mine and sidestepped me to look into the shower room. Once satisfied that there was room for me, he nodded for me to get to moving. Walking toward the indicated direction with as much dignity a naked man can muster under these circumstances, I broke eye contact and turned, starting to walk away when the ape called out that I would need this, giving me half a bar of hotel soap. I nodded my thanks and continued.

It couldn't have been any more than five feet from the exam point to the entrance of the shower room. I really didn't know what to expect, but I had visualized a shower room pretty much like the ones in school or even the military. Large enough to accommodate several to a half-dozen bodies. Rounding the corner brought to my eyes a sight to behold!

The construction of this room was planned for the productive efficiency of a "keep 'em moving and be quick about it" layout. The middle walkway was a raised grate of steel about five feet wide that extended to the exiting doorway. On each side of the grate was a six- to eight-inch step down, with a steel grate covering the drainage. The grates that I am describing were the kind that you find on sidewalks, through which you can see with the rectangular spaces. The shower area, to the best of my estimation, was about fifty feet in length. The walls were tiled, and spaced along the wall were five pipes on each side, yielding a total of ten bodies full capacity, but only seven men were currently in. Each one of the extended wall pipes had a make-shift showerhead attached to it. What was most noteworthy is that there was no faucet handles of any kind.

I stepped down onto the grate and went to one of the heads. Shoes called out, "Be quick, boy, because when the water stops, you get out." Hurriedly I soaped, then rinsed, in record time. While the water still ran, quickly I soaped my feet and groin area, and as I was rinsing, the water suddenly turned off. A call came from outside saying, "Next!" Each of us stepped from the floor onto the top grate, filing to the exit. Each, upon exiting, was given something—and I do mean *something*—to dry off with! Torn bedsheet, old undershirt, if lucky a towel, even some type of denim cloth. After discarding your drying tool into a large laundry basket on wheels, you were handed a top and bottom scrubs-style apparel. Walking barefoot, because socks were not provided, we continued down a corridor that dead-ended to the back of the building. There were four dorm-size partitioned rooms, each of which could hold thirty bodies apiece on fifteen bunk beds. Ahead of me, Shoes said, "Come on, boy. You, me, and Digger be bunking in the same room."

We went into the second dorm on the left and headed toward the back. Digger constantly greeted all that were already in, and Shoes directed me to select the top bunk on the back wall and he would be on the bottom. Digger took the bunk next to ours and held the top bunk by standing and leaning toward us. I understood that this was a preplanned strategic maneuver, because from our position our backs were covered by the wall and we could see in all directions. I climbed on the top bunk, swinging my feet over the edge, ensuring that his head wasn't at that end. Then I sat and watched the undertaking unfold. Through the sea of partially washed bodies, Hustle Man came through the door with searching eyes. Digger raised his hand, and he began to weave between the beds toward us. As he neared, Digger met him, and they paused and privately spoke. Then, with a nod, Digger weaved his way out of the room and Hustle Man came to and sat on the bottom bunk, which Digger had reserved with his presence, and by sitting he guarded the unattended top one. He and Shoes began speaking, and being that they weren't speaking directly to me, but about me, I remained silent and continued my vigilance of watching the crowd's interaction.

CHAPTER 11

Indoctrination

After a few minutes of their private powwow, Shoes asked me to come down and sit on his bunk. I hopped down and sat, and he and Hustle Man stood, with me sandwiched between them. Shoes explained that only one could be on a bunk at once but we could fraternize if others stood, just as long as it was no more than four in any conversation. That struck me as strange, but I made no comment.

With Shoes at one end of the bunk and Hustle Man at the other, so that both directions were being observed, for the first time, now that we had time, I knew Shoes was about to give me a full indoctrination of what was really going on.

"Boy, this here is Hustle Man. He is the reason you got in here tonight. He, like many others, serves purpose for the survival of all of us. We are a community, because no man can stand by hisself for very long against many. Everybody got a specialty. Hustle Man can barter and trade water to fish, and ice to Eskimos!" This brought a chuckle from the man being praised for his gaffing gifts. "You've met Digger. He got an eye and nose for things that most of us wouldn't give a shit about, but whatever he's drawn to is profitable to the tribe. You going to be meeting others, but for now we need to bring you up to speed so you don't stick out like a duck out of water."

"Now," he continued, "I heard that you met One-Eye Mary at the feed this afternoon. Be careful not to let her hear you call her One-Eye, because she always keeps that bat handy!" He said this with a wink, laugh, and shake of his head. I wondered if any of them had been used for batting practiced.

While I sat wondering that, Hustle Man chimed in, "Boy, don't worry about that 'Eat shit' comment. That's one of her favorites, and everybody gets it! She knows what you did for Shoes today, and she herself told us to make sure to get you to safety from them Clay boys. Hell, we would have done it anyway."

At that moment, I realized that I had been rescued by a well-organized operation that was cloaked in the appearance of the disadvantaged, and because of the social mindset of homelessness, it dismissed any type of intelligence! The perfect hiding spot is indeed in plain sight! My second thoughts rested on the woman with one eye. How did she fit into this absurd matrix of a world?

Shoes started again, "You remember what I told you this morning about the different sections of people wandering the streets?"

I answered, "Yes, sir."

That got a rise out of Hustle Man. "That's a respectful little cuss, ain't he, Shoes?"

Shoes's reply was a perfectly aimed answer: "That's just one of the reasons he's here."

Really, the time that I had spent in the wilds, I only thought briefly about why I was anywhere. The answer was always glaring: it was because of active addiction, alcoholism, and perhaps some type of secreted mental disorder that caused me to continually make sick choices with sick results. At one point, and I don't remember when it happened, I knew I was nothing but a two-bit wannabe hoodlum on the lam from the law. A junkie, a drunk, a deadbeat dad. A waste of gravity. So here and now, someone had just spoken that one of the reasons I was there was that I was a "respectful little cuss." I don't know why that hit me the way it did; I do know that it was significant, because I have never forgotten it. Again, one of many episodes seemingly unimportant in themselves and unrelated but monumental in the scheme of things.

Shoes continued, "A number of years ago, having spent a long time out West and Midwest, I was traveling the Eastern Seaboard and happened to be passing this way. At that time, tramps were just passing through on the rails and whatnot. Most of the time, Johnny Law would run them off or lock 'em up to prove what they called vagrancy. You couldn't really blame the townsfolk, because most of them tramps in that day were always spoiling the pickings because they were rowdy or just downright no account. It so happened a couple of little kids got messed up by a particularly racy bunch, and the town went on a vigilante mission. This began a war, if you could call it one, because we didn't have guns or reputation. It was a lost cause to plead innocent, because we were guilty of dereliction of social responsibility. Now, there were some kind do-gooders, but the die had been cast. It got so bad that some of the homeless began to go missing. This wasn't because they had moved on but because they were being killed systematically, their bodies hidden in the mines out yonder that had been closed down. On and off I'd leave, only to return to find the acts of vengeance on both sides kept increasing.

"One day, a friend of mine named Ned, a good-hearted old boy, got killed. The law didn't even investigate. Just like with a dog dead on the side of the road, they didn't send the coroner but sent a farmer in an old pickup truck and Bobcat to scoop Ned in the bucket and dump him into the truck. Boy, they didn't take him to a funeral home—they took him to a field and built a fire hot enough to burn him up, then scattered the ashes in the field!"

He continued after a pause, "You said you remember our talk today about the different groups of our people."

I nodded.

He went on. "I am one of the last true hobos. We are a breed of people that're beholden to no one but ourselves and God himself. I've always known the world was going to hell in a handbasket—that's why I quit it! However, seeing what was done to Ned, a good soul never having harmed anyone or anything, made me mad. I was mad at myself. You see, you can live this life for so long that a part of you dies. Sometimes it doesn't die quick, but it slowly moans and groans itself to death. I think what happened to me and what happened to Ned tore something away from me, something that had eroded away. What it was was being a human being! Even though I wasn't much one before, I was indeed human! Today, you showed me—all of us, for that matter—we have a right to life. Boy, you got to be careful not to forget you are human, though you choose to live below what they call human standards. Though we may choose a different life from most, still we got the right. Now, we've surrendered our rights to demand rights as they are, yes, but we still have dignity, pride. So stand as tall as any other man. If we abide by the law, keep to ourselves, and hold value to others and respect them, then they should allow us to live in peace. Most of the time, we accept our invisibility. That's natural. However, to punish us, harm us, or kill us? That's wrong! Son, there is no justice. It's *just us*."

"There is no justice. It's *just us*," echoed in my head and found a place deep within my own imposed misery as a true statement.

He was then silent as he looked into the distant past, and Hustle Man stood silently, nodding in sorrowful agreement. I remained silent. I knew that when he was ready, he would give me the "for real for real" reason for this discussion. And I didn't have to wait very long.

Shoes continued in a low, measured voice, and I didn't have trouble hearing him over the dim surrounding conversations. He was like a snake charmer; I was enrapt with the flutelike quality of his voice.

"Years ago, an unofficial truce was met between the townsfolk and the transients. Earlier today, I gave you the lowdown on the various classes of homeless. Well, after the Great Depression, and even before to some degree, there have always been what they call the bums in the street. However, the Great Depression brought the vagabonds up close and personal. Hell, around that time, most of America were on the skids, and people that were always normal fell when the system failed. Many, from what I understand, took to suicide. So it's no wonder that most commoners are afraid of us, because one missed paycheck then it's out on the streets for them too! Since that time in America's historic downfall, all kinds of money and politics have been applied to clean America up and not let what happened ever happen again. Of course, it's to no happy end. People are still afraid, and the homeless are still among them. It's like a constant reminder that nothing's a for-sure thing.

"Anyway, I told you that some came through here and caused all kinds of damage throughout time. Believe me when I tell you this: we don't hold nothing against them folks for the way they behave. We try to keep them from being afraid of us, by acting human and docile. We make sure not to be a nuisance or to cause disturbances, and we pick litter up and wash the outside windows for free. In other words, boy, what I am saying is that we ain't trying to overthrow their teachings of what is acceptable and we abide by their law because it's their land."

I had never considered this train of thought. I was certain that no one outside of these types of people could have come up with such an amicable type of philosophy that bridged the impossible expanse of the American dream to that of a hobo substandard. His toned inflection let me know that anything that was going to be spoken from this point was going to carry a heavy weight with it.

"In all societies, there are taboos that must not happen. When violations of these core sacred tenets are committed, anything like normal punishment is thrown to the winds. What happens is that we see the evil that men are truly capable of leap from their mind to actively become the living horror that they are in broad daylight!"

I shivered at this lead-in.

"When anything happens to womenfolk or children, that disrupts all that man calls holy and something got to be done to right the wrong. This includes the fact that the innocent, being conveniently at hand, can and will be used as blood sacrifice for revenge!"

He went on after a short pause. "What happened to Ned shouldn't have happened to neither man nor beast. He was guilty of one thing and one thing only: he was not part of the established normal system. He was guilty because of association. I took it hard. I took it so hard I was no longer afraid for myself or what anyone might do to me, even though I was nothing but another bum in the street. I left town and I went farther south. Being that I had traveled for years and had been part of many tribes, I had people I knew all over. Now was the time to use our vast network for something other than just to find handouts, jobs, and safe havens. This time it was to save our world and our way of life. One thing you're going to find out, boy, is that information on the rails can find anybody and is more accurate than all news in the paper and TV."

Concluding that statement brought a low "Amen" from Digger.

"All along the way, I met up with others and spread the word about the approximate times this evil was being done, and for eyes and ears to be open for the perpetrators that caused this mess. I don't know, but I think I was gone about a month, and during this time I was spreading the word and receiving information about similar things in other places. Slowly word started to get more specific. There was talk of a band of tramps who, it seemed, every time they'd show up, some type of real trouble happened. In all this, when they left, it appeared the trouble stopped. As a matter of fact, I had come upon them once but didn't sit for coffee or drink with them, simply because I was on such an important mission. I'm quite sure it would have been the end of me if I had sat a spell with them. They would have figured out that I was aiming to find who had set all this shit into motion and would have the tribal leaders weigh in on their asses. We have a justice system too, boy, and it's a far cry better than what them folk call justice!"

Again, Digger weighed in with a gibberish comment, but it was Hustle Man's comment that stuck with me: "Ain't nothing worse than a damn tramp being trampy!"

Shoes went to declare that he was saved by divine intervention. "Ain't nothing but God that did that!" he said. "I was so riled up by the children, the fear of the townsfolk, the tribe being destroyed, and Ned's killing that I lost the thing that had kept me alive all these years. And that's being observant, seeing things that appear to be okay but being able to see that they really are not! Boy, you are going to have to develop that sense if you're going to stay alive."

Digger and Hustle Man both nodded, and the vigilant watch had now ceased, with only an occasionally glance around the perimeter.

"Hey, Digger, you remember that fellow that used to ride with Ned?" asked Shoes.

"Yeah, that White boy Josie. I think he was an albino, 'cause he was so white and Ned so black we used to call them Ebony and

Ivory." With that, he smiled one of those types when you remember a fond memory.

"Yeah, that's him. I couldn't call his name, but I remember how destroyed he was when Ned got killed. I really think that he and Ned were a little more than traveling companions," said Shoes thoughtfully.

"Hell, Shoes, everyone knew that! Ned said he was going to marry his snowflake as soon as they could find a place that they could live in peace," came the comment of general knowledge by Hustle Man.

"Well, I guess dead is the place for that. I mean, peace and all," commented Digger.

Hustle Man looked at Digger. "Nigger, you really fucked you. No respect for the dead!"

"I got respect for the dead. He was my friend too! I didn't mean anything by it. Just ain't anybody disturbing the dead," Digger replied woefully.

I had to admit he was right, but I knew better than to get involved with that.

The following came on its heel from Hustle Man to Digger. "Friends like you, a man don't need enemies!" Having said that, he turned to Shoes and asked him to go on. "And please don't involve Digger in the telling of it."

"Fuck you!" And off through the dorm Digger went.

Shoes watched the verbal warriors in quiet amusement, and I could see just how dear his tribe (family) was to him, and how their banter had relieved some of the intensity of his pain of the past days. For a few moments, we watched as Digger traveled and spoke to others, and we knew for certain that he was digging up something by his animated posture and conspiratorial conversations. I smiled, Shoes shook his head, and Hustle Man laughingly said, "I know he's digging up something to drink!"

CHAPTER 12

Mary's Revenge

I thought that maybe the conversation would pick back up at another time, but as Digger was leaving our designated area, Shoes began on a different line.

"Back in the day, Mary had two eyes and anyone with eyes was looking at her. Under all those clothes is a fine woman! Plus, she's smart as a whip. It's said that Mary worked in the banking field and got some good education. I know she reads well and has no problem communicating. You really wouldn't know that, though, as much as she tells everyone to eat shit! But believe me, there's nothing dull about her," Shoes said. "Well, as for me, I can tell you what I've seen of her and how she spoke."

I wasn't going to do any investigation on what Shoes was saying. When you mention Mary to me, I think *bat*—they're one and the same to me!

"We figured out who was who and knew that the band of hoodlums would circle back, because they were known as pickers. *Pickers* are some of us that get work around crop season. Sometimes it's tater fields, tobacco, cucumbers, peaches, apples, oranges, and whatnot. In those days, the Clay boys were really little boys, but their old man, who's dead now, was a trifling piece of flesh. Word had it that one of those goons that you messed up with today was actually a nephew." I must have looked surprised, because Shoes continued as though all this was common fact. "It used to be four kids by that scum, but he went to messing with his daughter and she got knocked up. The mama couldn't take that, along with the beatings, and it was said she went to her people in Tennessee and was to send for the kids. Naw, that didn't happen, and the boys grew thinking that they were all brothers. They were always in some kind of mess, and it's certain that if there was anything wrong, they had something to do with it. Long story short, the girl got killed in a boyfriend's car, and the boys, who were almost grown then, stayed with that miserable cuss until he died."

Digger, just breezing in from whatever hustling and scheming, interjected, "Damn him, he got what he deserved, screaming and yelling shit wouldn't leave him alone. Ghost and demons. I think it was cancer or something to do with all that drinking!"

Shoes replied, "No matter what the cause, it was a hell of a way to go. The boys stayed on and were into every kind of mischief, later doing county and state time. It was during one of their stays at a county or state facility that I decided it was best to act. Those scoundrel boys were always harassing us, so it would be best not to have to contend with their nonsense while we were at some real work! Me and the tribe had decided to set the trap for those tramp mofos. Mary, looking like she did back then, said she'd be the bait. What we needed was to get them in some spot that no one could see or hear. I tell you this, boy: When it comes to hobo justice, there's no middle of the road. That's because the road we travel on is so narrow.

"It was late summer, when all pickers normally begin to make their way to where they know work is to be had. Most of the time, the farmers and produce companies know them from the times they had worked for them before. It's a pretty good gig for all. The growers and produce companies pay very little, and the pickers get housing, shelter, pay, and dope and alcohol, all at the same place, right there on those patches of land that they work on, and they got no worries from Johnny Law as long as they stay put. Once in a while, however, that ain't enough for them and they sneak off for some town excitement or pussy. No matter how you cut it, it never ends well. Mary had both eyes back then but was eager to get those bastards, so we plotted out the works of making it happen. Her and an ole boy named Jax got on at one of those camps. We sent them in as a couple, not married, but together. You see, when on the road, you lay claim to someone as married, that starts a problem of how to get rid of the body. This is opposed to if it's a boyfriend-girlfriend thing. It is only a matter of showing who the best pick is. Now, before you ask me what's the difference, just know that we regard certain things certain ways, and that's all there is to it.

"Sure enough, they got to a camp and two of that crew were there, and Mary found out that the other three were at another field place. Here's what we did: Mary, being a looker, real faintly began to make flirts so as not to alarm anyone or cause any outright fighting. After about a week, me and some of the boys caught up to two of those fellas as they were heading to town on a Friday. And that was the last anybody heard from them. This don't cause no alarms, because during the picking season, niggers come and go. We told Jax to hop camp and go keep an eye on that other knucklehead left by himself. That totally opened the door for those two creeps that'd been sneaking candies, liquor, and all to Mary behind her old man's back. Didn't take long for them to turn up the heat and begin asking her what she going to do. She pretended that she planned to meet up with her old man and they'd be heading south for the winter."

Shoes fell silent for a moment, so I seized the moment to ask, "Shoes, you said these men were the ones that started the trouble."

"Yeah, they were the ones. So what are you saying?" he challenged.

There was no backing out. "How did you know?" I looked questioningly at him.

"Boy, one of those little girls had a necklace that her daddy had given to her, and when they dragged those babies in the bushes, that necklace was never found, until one of those jugheads had it around his neck. On top of that, some of the network were drinking with a couple of them, and after being juiced a bit, they started talking about their crew's dark adventure. You see, to them any wrong that they did to the White man was justified. Hell, ain't they the ones that stole us from Africa and sold us into slavery? When one of the hobos said that was sick thinking, they beat him almost to death. That nigger with the necklace kept saying, 'Once you got Blacked, you never go back!' No doubt, they the ones, and this time God would use the hand of man to punish them."

I looked into his eyes and had no doubt that he believed then, and probably still believes it to this day, that he was appointed judge, jury, and executioner.

"Day finally came when Mary set them up on the same day. She told one that she'd meet him by that brook in the wooded area by the trains at a certain time. The other, she told him she'd meet him in the woods outside of town. That was where we had met the other two fellers I told you about two weeks before. The tribe split up into two groups, each heading to the spots long before the meeting times. We didn't want Mary to get hurt, but we definitely wanted to make sure those plague of humans was stopped."

I remember how when he said *plague*, my mind went straight to the Bible, as it spoke of plagues in Egypt and the end of times.

"The first meeting went off without a hitch. Sure enough, the nigger was there—had even washed up before he got there! Mary came through the brush and ran up to him, telling him all sorts of stuff about how she been watching him closely and how long she been waiting to get with him. That was truer than anything else she said. She told him to close his eyes, which he did, and she unbuckled his pants, all the time whispering loud enough how much she was going to enjoy this. Boy, listen up, no way did we plan to have Mary get into any of the dirt when dealing with those pigs, but she had other ideas. With his eyes still closed, she took his pecker in her hands and began to pump him till it was standing like a flagpole. Before any of us could even think about how to get at him, Mary pulled a straight razor out of her tits and sliced the damn thing off right up to the hairs! It was so quick we, or he, never knew what happened! When the blood squirted, that nigger went screaming, and I'm thinking, he screamed worse than those terrified babies they dragged into the bushes. As he was backing up, trying to stop the bleeding, Mary stood up with his dick in her hand, smiling calmly at him. We had to rush him and quiet him, and when we got him down, she walked up to him and, looking down on him, with his johnson in her hand, said, 'Eat shit, mofo.' And then threw his dick on his face. Boy, she sent chills through me! Even though all of us one day are going to have to answer to our Maker for what we done, I don't think he'll ever mention it to Mary. I know none did or ever will! For all that bloodletting, she didn't have any blood on her but her hands, which caused me to think mayhap this ain't her first castration!

"The second setup wasn't as smooth as we hoped for. Mary got there before, and when that spook showed up, he was like a bull in heat. He was mad because he knew Mary had set him and his boy up on the same day to give pussy to. He didn't know that his pussy days were now numbered. She tried explaining that she had to be sure of what was best for her, but the more she tried to calm him down, the more he got riled up. The tough part about this was that the other part of the tribe wasn't at the right spot. You see, this ole boy was so fumed that he met Mary before she could get to the spot, so everything was already fucked before it started. So what I'm telling you is what she had to say about what happened before we could get there. It was some dark and ugly business that needed concluding that day. He snatched at her and was going to take what he felt was rightfully his. Breaking away from him, she started talking real loud, trying to alert us. Now, we could still hear her and were heading, backtracking to them. Apparently, he made to grasp at her, and out of her tit case came that straight razor, cutting his arm. That made him damn near unstoppable in rage. He punched her and knocked her to the ground, and he kicked her in the ribs a couple of times. Now she was really screaming. I could hear it! Fear and rage took us.

"Mary slashed blindly at him and took off running into the woods, and he ran after her. All this led them farther away from us. That nigger picked up a rock or something and threw it at her, and sure enough, it found its mark, catching her in the back of the head and neck. When she fell forward, it was on the wooded floor, and that was where one of several small branches had fallen sometime before, in the right place and position. She fell directly on it, and that was how she lost her eye. The doc said that if it had been any longer or if there was more force, she'd probably have died. As it was, she had gotten to her knees, crying, while he was kicking her in the ass, calling her whore and whatnot. Saying he was going to get that ass.

When we got to where they were, he had had Mary's dress hiked up in the back and she was bent over some deadfall. He was ripping her drawers off when the first club met his nappy head.

"Mary hadn't been the same since that day, and the only recollection, I believe, she may have of that day is her moment of shining glory: 'Eat shit, mofo.' I tell you this, boy: I feel responsible for Mary losing that eye, and God knows I'd give her my sight if I could. I think that wound did affect her brain too, because after that shit went down, she started wearing her clothes the way that you see her today. It was slow, these changes, but they were noticeable even back then. It only goes to show that no good deed goes unpunished!"

CHAPTER 13

Invitation

It was dead quiet when Shoes said that last statement. And it wasn't because the murmuring backdrop of sound had stopped. No, I realized that I had visually been transported back to those days of yore. I can't explain it—I couldn't then, and I can't today—why I remember some roads as vividly as I do others in haze, and still yet others, none at all. This is just one of many that I do.

When I realized that the telling was complete, I looked about me, as if trying to come out of some type of dream. It appeared the telling of this particular history affected all of us within the listening circle, but differently on deeper personal levels. I remembered then that Shoes had said some type of truce was called. But I didn't remember in my dream state experiencing when a truce had been mentioned! "Shoes," I said, "you said something about a truce between the tribe and the townsfolk. Did I miss something?"

"Dummy, that was the truce!" yelled Digger.

"What?" I exclaimed.

"Taking care of those assholes was the truce. Damn, Shoes, that boy ain't ever going to get to hobo style!"

"Wait a minute. Hold up. Okay, you saying the truce was to get the perpetrators. I can follow that. But I can't wrap my mind around how you could prove these fellas were the ones and that the deed was done."

"Damn, ya'll, that boy is slower than my grandma—and she's been dead a long time!" commented Hustle Man.

I rolled me eyes at each of the older men, though I did not make any comments or show any agitation at their ribbing of my intelligence. I did posture that I could wait until they finally decided to give up the required information that would fit all the puzzle pieces together.

Finally, Shoes picked up on the story to bring closure.

"All along, we been sending messages to the county sheriff. At that time, it was a cracker by the name of Wilcox. Wilcox was a good ole boy who loved his beer and whores. The only reason he took the job was for the money and pension. In those days, the town wasn't rowdy and pretty much took care of itself. Wilcox didn't mind the tramps, because he was able to get federal money by having our names on the town and county payroll. As long as we stayed out of sight and didn't have any problems having our names used bogusly and in fattening his personal finances, he left us alone. Only on occasion would we have to pitch in to do any work. Christmas decorations and other holidays or big-event trash pickup."

I figured that explained why the folks spoke to the underprivileged. I could only shake my head in amazement.

"It was good business for everyone. Well, you can imagine the horror when your dog is rabid and starts to attack the master's house. The dog got to be put down! You can always get another dog, but it ain't as easy for the dog to get another master," he continued. "It may take one, two years to build the makings of a town, city, or any kind of society, but it takes a whole bunch of years for a place to accept the rubbish of the world in their own backyard. That was why the outhouses were always farthest from the house, because of the smell of shit." He smiled. "We told Wilcox that ain't none of the locals had nothing to do with it and done put word out. He said he couldn't do nothing about the townsfolk's action and he wasn't going to jail any of them. He also said that the person wasn't supposed to know that we were working on it and that it be best if he got the credit." He paused. "Boy, there is no backup. It's always all or nothing. You couldn't blame the sheriff, though. We were, and are still, nothing in their eyes. Normally, that's just fine, because we're left in peace to go through our own personal suffering."

I reflected on this while yet again he paused. In my mind I could never have imagined the intricate patterns that governed the world of hobos and tramps. From the outside looking in, it gave all appearances of a life free of obligations and worry. What slowly dawned in my understanding was that this chosen life was not for the weak of heart or the stupid!

"Wilcox would feed us information that he was getting from the surrounding areas. Sometimes he'd run us in on trumped-up vagrancy charges and keep us a day or two, feeding us information, and us giving him the same. By this time, the little girls' families had moved, but the issue of that necklace was never released publicly. That was one fact. The other was the confession of one of those assholes when they thought they were safe, and the third thing was, the police reporting was the same where similar things happened. God only knows why nobody connected the dots. Might just be White folk and rich folk just need protecting from their own, or themselves. In the end, we let him know where to find them and left the necklace in the one's hand and dumped them where Ned had died. Wilcox called all the other agencies, making it appear that he had found the links, then followed up by retracing where that gang had been in other spots that had had trouble. It made headlines that vigilantes had done it, so the law was looking for them for taking the law in their hands. Of course, they weren't looking very hard for one of their own who was only defending his community. In fact, they were secret heroes. Besides, imagine the cost that it would have raised to bring those shit birds to justice and then house, feed, and take care of them. Wilcox was declared some type of top investigator and offered a job in a decent-size city for more money. Most things did return, gradually, back to normal. The only thing that didn't was our Mary."

The silence that ensued in the telling of this tale was palpable, and the air thickened, almost akin to breathing underwater. Time, for all practical reasons, had stopped, and I was stuck in the aftermath of the story that had been told. I understood that it was the prelude to something else. Why would anyone recount something like this to a complete stranger? It didn't give me the feeling of being sworn to secrecy, nor did it give me the feeling that anything was wanted or warranted from me. What was a certainty was that another interlude was being introduced. My head did not hurt, but it was full. Images, noises, thoughts, and a series of all of today's events raced and trolled in my head.

Through the midst of thinking and feeling, I became aware that Shoes had been softly calling to me. As my eyes began to focus in the here and now, he leaned down to me, with Digger and Hustle Man standing by.

"Boy," he said, "listen to me. I told some things so that you can know you are no longer on the outside looking in but are now in it—tramphood, hoboism, or as they call it today, homelessness. To be able to live on the road, and if you should find your way out of it back into mainstream society, there are things you really need to know. Especially if you're going to not only survive but also live and thrive. Many lose their way, their minds, their health, and even their will to exist. If you don't want that, then you gonna have to do some learning. I'm asking you to consider hanging with us awhile. I know you be heading south, but I'm asking you to hold up for a little while. You see, I owe you for what you did today. Hell, any one of us back in the day would have done it. You brought us hope. You brought the memory of real solidarity and dignity to those of us that have been on these fringes for many a lifetime. Stay with us so we can give you life lessons. These won't just be for you but for others too. One day— and I really pray that you do—you'll find your way off this world. These same life lessons work in the real world too!"

So this was the reason for his taking the time to tell me the story and give me an explanation for things. Yes, I was heading south, and I was certainly trying to get down there before the first snowflake hit the ground. Additionally, I had to admit, today was definitely an adventure, and I did learn things that had never before entered into my conscious mind. And these pointed-out observations were always directly in the front for me and all the world to see. The big question was, Why didn't I know about them? And if I didn't recognize these things, how much more could or would I and all people not see?

Hustle Man said, "Boy, light's gonna be out in 'bout fifteen minutes, so you better make up your mind."

I stared at him in crystal clear vision. I turned my head to look directly in his eyes and said, "I'll walk with yinz awhile."

"Good. About a month or so, I'll be migrating south, and we can walk a bit more together," Shoes said. "Climb on up and get some sleep. We be leavin' out of here about six in the morning."

I had stood to give him his bunk back and to hoist to the top one when Digger nudged me and said, "Here, take a good swallow of this. It'll help you sleep." He said this as he winked at me. In his hand he held out a small plastic bottle that contained a liquid looking like grape juice. Having already sipped from his mystery bottles today, I prepared myself for the impact of the drink. He said, "Big swallow, boy!"

I sat back on the bottom bunk and tilted the elixir, taking a walloping gulp. The pungent order was in my nose, and the thick nip, much thicker than today's, had my cheeks bulging. It took two swallows to clear my mouth. I stood after I handed him the bottle back, just as the liquid hit my stomach. Unlike the fiery burn of the mouth, throat, and stomach today, there was a slow-coating sensation and smooth, okay feeling that followed. He slapped me on the back, saying, "That will help tonight. You won't mind the farts, the snoring, or the night screams."

The effect of the drink was immediate, though it was possible that today's events added to its potency, or at least so I thought. Later, I would find that this was a special blend, specifically mixed and measured for "mission nights."

As I began my climb to the top, bunk the dorm lights began to flicker on and off. From the hallway we could hear the ape-man say, "Lights-out!" The flickering continued until everyone made it to their assigned bunks and quieted. I stretched out under the wool blanket, which didn't cover my feet, and decided to turn on my side in a semifetal position to completely cover them. With my body relaxing and the race inside my head rolling to a gentle stop, I heard in the quiet rustling of covers, "Good night, Michael," from Shoes on the lower bunk. I murmured what I thought might have been a "Good night," but God only knows.

What still sticks with me is that I did smile at the thought that he had said my name. I had been "boy" all, day and now the last word of the day was my very own name! Damn, I owned a day, and that was the end of my day.

CHAPTER 14

Learning the Ropes

I slept, just as Digger had said. The noises, night screams, and farts never disturbed my rest. Coming to, I found that the lights were already on. Though there was small movement in the dorm, most of the occupants were still in the bunks, but you knew that they were just lying there to grab a few moments before the start of the day.

Shoes called from below, "Boy, did you sleep pretty good?" I answered that I did. While answering him, I glanced at the bottom bunk across from him. I saw on the top bunk Digger, but I couldn't figure out the heap of clothing under the thin blanket on the bunk below his.

As more of the men began to move about and the morning movements increased, I rose and stretched while in a sitting position. Of course, the tales that were told the previous night still hung on the fringes of my mind. I decided to table them, knowing that to dwell on all that information would make for a long day. Checking to ensure that my feet would not be in Shoes's face, I swung down to the floor. Shoes, I noticed, was pulling up a pair of socks on his feet then. Now that I was at floor level, I again looked at the covered figure in the bunk. Shoes steadily watched me and then spoke.

"That's Mary. We got an arrangement."

This having said, the statement was the final answer to any question that I might have had. I just nodded and looked about the room as Digger began his morning ritual of loudly yawning, smacking his sunken cheeks, and scratching his head vigorously as he sat

102

up. He then hopped down with practiced ease and greeted me and Shoes. He looked at Mary's slumbering form next, and with a nod to no one except himself, he quickly headed toward the exit of the dorm.

From behind me Shoes spoke. "Many of the times that we decide to come to the mission, Mary, of course, goes with the women and children. However, during the course of the night, she makes her way to where I or Digger may be. We always save the bottom bunk for her," he said. "Everybody knows, and nobody says anything, and we keep it quiet. I think she feels safe, and we rest good knowing that as long as she is with us, she is safe. Now, I don't know how she does this, but she does, and don't be no fool to question it. You might just get that bat upside your head!" He chuckled, and I chuckled as well. "Come on, boy. Leave her lying. She'll be along when she comes." His eyes lingered for a moment on the slumbering figure, and I, even in my rough state of mind, could see tenderness and affection on his face.

We weaved our way through the mass of bodies toward the doorway, where our belongings were stored. Handing the attendant our tickets of identification, we got our belongings and started to dress. While I laced my shoes, I heard Shoes say, "Digger will be getting us some breakfast and more. We're going to head on out now." Without questioning Mary's appearance in the men's dorm or how Digger was going to get us breakfast or what *more* meant, I followed his lead.

Outside, the start of a beautiful day was captured by the rising streaks of sunlight and the fresh smell of the open air and the sounds of distant dogs barking and birds chirping. I looked about the street. Once again, it was still asleep, and other than an occasional passing vehicle, it remained abandoned. All was quiet and all was well at this time of day, before the worries it brought and the haunts of yesterday could take hold.

"Today you're going to start learning the ropes. I've already talked with Digger and a few others. We taking you under our wings for a while. Since you going to stick a while, might as well teach you, so you can be of some use to us and yourself. You ain't got a problem learning some things, do you, boy?"

"No, sir."

"Good, because like I told you, I'll be heading south and we can head out together before any snow. And it will be easier for both of us if we both are up to snuff."

The rest of the walk was in silence, only interrupted by the greetings that Shoes spoke and responded to. I recognized the direction we were headed to. We were beelining to the alleyway that we had come to yesterday to clean. Once we were in the alley, Shoes proceeded to the metal door of the kitchen and we were greeted by the kitchen worker. The buckets of soapy water were brought out, and we began the cleaning of the alley.

About halfway through, Shoes began, "I have one of our own coming by, and you're going to head out with him. He's a good man. You might think he's kind of strange, though, but don't worry none. He's the best."

Listening, I remained silent. I kept thinking, Was it even possible to think anyone or anything could be considered strange? Especially after all the encounters that one mere day had produced yesterday! No, I was thinking that anything I might consider normal would definitely be strange! So when a squat-statured man showed up with a small wooden wagon and began talking to Shoes, that was the definition of *normal*. I continued to work as we had yesterday, until I was called over to meet this "normal" character.

"Boy, this here is Mixer," Shoes said. "You'll go with him until Digger or I come get you. I'll wrap this up and head toward some other business."

Without another word to Shoes or me, he turned as the wheels low-squeaked, heading to the street. I gathered my shirt and followed. We walked several blocks, the only conversation between us coming from the squeaking wheels of the wagon. It was made of wood and was painted blue, red, yellow, black, green, and white. No rhyme, no reason, just splotches of color, all over the wagon. Except for the squeaky wheels, the wagon was sturdy and looked to be well-kept.

"Boy, I'm Mixer. You and me got some rounds to make. I work at a couple of the bars, clean up and all. That gets us a little money and quite a bit to drink. You got to know that at bars is one of the places we get information. Information is *more precious* than all the gold in the world. By itself, it ain't shit. Most folk will disagree! However, without action, information just lies still. Boy, you got to know, to use information, you got to move on it when you supposed to, or you'll lose anything you're trying to get into the right position. You understand what I'm putting down?" Mixer started the conversation so suddenly that, at first, I didn't know if he was really talking to me or, like Digger, talking to himself.

I said, "It makes sense to me."

Without my knowing whether or not my answer was received, we continued our journey up the street.

We were by then approaching a street across from the park where Digger had woken me up and given me the shoes when the short man stopped and turned to finally face me. I held my ground to await whatever was coming. What did come wasn't what I expected; he motioned me to the park area, and we sat on a bench. The day, being mild and sunny, was warm and gentle. We sat and looked as the squirrels flittered on the grounds and limb-hopped from tree to tree. Mixer pulled the watch cap from his head and reached in his back pocket to pull a snot-rag, dabbing it at his perspiring forehead. After a few more moments, he said, "You know, boy, when sometimes I sit and watch quiet-like and see all that God made, I think and feel that it is beautiful. I wish I could hold on to that moment always, but somehow or another, I keep losing it. Then it appears again and I try to hold it, but I wind up losing it. It happens over and over, but it always comes back, just to stay awhile. You know what I think those moments really are?"

Whether it was a rhetorical question or just an out-loud thought, I knew in my bones that I was required to say something. So I asked reverently, "Mr. Mixer, what do you think those moments really are?"

I'll never forget the look in his eyes and his countenance when he responded, "Those are times when God himself comes to let me know, no matter what, he hasn't forgotten me. He don't send angels, he don't even send his Son, but he rises from his throne and says, 'I will go see my child Mixer.'"

That had an impact on me. At that time, it was so powerful that chills and goose bumps came over me. Not the type that sent shivers through one's body, but a warmth and comfort at such a thought that was simply put to words. This was just one of many! This was an instance that stirred something within me that was significant and yet unexplainable. Today, I recognize this as a seed of hope that was planted.

We sat awhile longer, and without any prompting from me, he said, "'Bout twelve thirty, the first joint is going to open. We need to be there for trash takeout and fix everything up for opening. Stay close to me, keep yo mouth shut, and act dumb. That shouldn't be too hard." He said the last jokingly, which I wouldn't have taken offense to if he had meant it. What I had figured out was that, hell, I really didn't know much about anything, and in all probability, I would leave this earth as dumb as a box of rocks!

We got up and headed across the street. The day was heading to a glorious late-summer day, and everything seemed to be as it should be, and I a part of it.

During the period of learning the ropes, I had the opportunity to meet members of this band of vagabonds. I found them to be highly organized, thoughtful, caring, and most of all, evolved in the highest degree of intellect and human understanding. Most of all, the names, amazingly, were monocles, each depicting exactly what they were as contributors of our guarded society! Shoes, because, though it was unknown to anyone how he got his money, every couple of months he'd get a new pair of brogans and give the worn but usable ones to others so that their feet could be cared for. Digger, since he had the ability to find treasure among the heaps of discards to financially assist the tribe. Hustle Man, for he retrieved and distributed accurate information and bartered and traded with townsfolk, merchants, and even the police department! Mixer, the one I was assigned with today, because he provided the drinks for the gatherings and was able to get dark secrets that were not common knowledge. Fixer was an individual that worked with anything, from electrical hookups and carpentry to stonework, brickwork, or block work. There were others, but of course, time, as with all things, has eroded much of my detailed memory. Yet the vibrant colors of these individuals still give gaiety to my somewhat-feeble mind. Believe it or not, we had our own "doctor," casually referred to as Doc. Doc was a Creole Indian, and many thought that he was a shaman type of witch doctor from Louisiana. He knew of plants, trees, medicines, and ancient cures. Mary was his fill-in nurse, and they spent much time together scavenging the wooded areas and the dumpsters behind the drugstores for ingredients for his elixirs.

What I do remember is that this society had a better systematic approach to equality and equity of individuals' right to live freely and be measured only by the content of their character than the mainstream society. I saw a community that thrived in perilous times and lived in peace with other communities. Not once did I witness aggression because of personal philosophies or spiritual beliefs. Not one other time in all my travels had I met such peaceable and sharing people as these. At this present time, I will not go into much more detail of the personalities and day-to-day lessons of my learning the ropes. Those were intense times filled with wonder, with me absolutely coming face-to-face with myself and the core beliefs that I had developed prior to this schooling. In the final analysis, what may be gleaned is that a divine act of providence smiled down on a misdirected fool and had mercy on him. These untouchables were assigned as my guardian angels, and no matter what anyone should say to agree or disagree, as Rhett Butler said to the beautiful Scarlett in the closing scene of *Gone with the Wind*, "Frankly, my dear, I don't give a damn."

As Mixer and I crossed the street, we headed once again to an alleyway behind the establishment. I had come to understand that alleys were part of the unspoken truce between the two factions of society. We did not approach an expected dumpster as I thought but stood beside a pile of wooden and cardboard boxes. "Boy, we begin with the cardboard, and while you go through it, don't crush it yet to fit flat in yonder dumpster. You got to see if it's strong enough to carry anything in it. Don't dump out any of the bottles you find."

I said nothing and just followed his lead.

We went through all the cardboard. The pieces that were already flat, I placed in the dumpster. Boxes, large and small, that I deemed sturdy, I set aside. We had about thirty bottles lined up along the wall, and as I looked at them, Mixer knew a question was coming.

"Now comes the trick with a hole in it," he said. I looked at him expectantly. "Go look in that box there and see if you can find anything that will hold liquid. Make sure it ain't got no holes in it!" For the second day in a row, I was climbing into yet another dumpster. I found several buckets of various sizes and stacked them. From outside I heard him say, "See if you see any old clothes or rags in there and bring them too. If not, newspaper will do."

I gathered what I could find and climbed from the space. Once I had carried the requested to the end we were working, Mixer explained that now we were going to go through the wooden cartons and pretty much do the same thing. Further, he said, when we had gotten the wood together with all the boxes that we had stacked, I should put all the bottles in them and move it all behind the dumpster until we had finished preparations inside and outside of the dive drinking hole. All this took about twenty to thirty-nine minutes, and satisfied with what we had don, he pronounced, "Now we got to head in. Remember, be quiet and act stupid."

He turned from me and walked a few feet to the door and banged loudly on it. From inside first I heard nothing, then I heard a raspy voice yell, "Who's that!"

"Mixer!" The reply, just as loud, was uttered.

Bolts were thrown back and locks turned, a crossbar removed, as the heavy combination of wood and metal overlay swung open and hit the brick wall. "Hell, Mixer, what time is it?"

"What I need a watch for? Time is all the same!" said Mixer as he stepped through the hole. He motioned for me to come in. The hallway was dark, and my eyes were still adjusting from being outside. Evidently, the man must have noticed me, because Mixer added as an afterthought, "This here is the boy. He hanging with me a few days, till we can get him on to his mommy."

I'm introduced as boy, I thought, *and I'm only here long enough so that they can get me to my mommy!*

On a positive note, at least I wasn't an orphan and stupid! Well, I was told not to say anything and to act stupid, so that was exactly what I did, and the man said nothing to me and accepted what Mixer had to say as gospel. We then moved into the bar area. As with most seedy drinking holes, the place was dimly lit, was dusty, and smelled of stale beer, liquor, and the hint of nausea of some type of aftermath. It had a small raised stage and an PA system for entertainment. Actually, it looked as though it was all ready to go.

Mixer said, "Boy, go back behind the bar and start getting those trash barrels emptied. Just pull those big bags out if you can. If not, give me a holler and I'll come help you. I'm going to get broom, dustpan, and vacuum."

When I crossed the floor to head behind the bar, there was a cat. Orange, with dark markings I couldn't make out. It was lying on one of the barstools, and I hadn't noticed it before. When I saw it, I stopped in surprise and made some kissing sounds to let it know that it didn't have to worry about me. The cat didn't move as I moved closer. Looking at its prone position, I assessed it was rather large and old. The animal was lying on its back, just like a dog, waiting for someone to rub its belly, and there were popcorn and peanut shells scattered in its fur. Its head was hanging from the stool in an awkward canter, and by all practical reasoning, it appeared to be dead, so still and nonmoving. Rounding the bar, I saw the barrels that were mentioned and began to gather the tops of the plastics inside of them. Mixer had returned only with a broom and started evenly spacing the chairs around the small tables. I pulled out the plastic covering of one of the cans; most of the contents were bottles.

Hearing the sound of the clanking bottles, Mixer said, "Boy, look here. Let's you and me work those trash barrels. What's in them is what we be looking for."

At the same time, I told him that I believed the cat to be dead. He replied that it was Clyde and that he was probably drunk and that he was a standing member of the bar. I said no more.

Mixer came behind with me and told me to go rinse one of the bar buckets out before we did anything else. Grabbing one of the three five-gallon buckets, I could see that they were used as receptacles for liquid waste from the bar. Bringing the rinsed container back, I was told to get another big bag and to start emptying each bottle's content into the bucket and placing the empty ones into the large plastic bag, I did as I was told and soon emptied all the bottles. After this maneuver had been completed, I was told to drag the other barrel beside it and do the same with its bottles. However, this time the bottles were placed into the previously emptied barrel. I did this three times and had collected almost four gallons of leftover drinks, their remnants. From what I could see in the slurry solution, it was apparent that liquid wasn't the only thing that I had collected. Cigarette butts, peanuts, popcorn, napkins, and a host of unidentifiable floaters were on the top!

When I completed the task, I called to Mixer, who, by this time, had found the vacuum cleaner and was noisily running it on the threadbare carpet. He looked up out of the dust cloud and said, "If you got room in that bucket for more, run outside and start dumping those bottles in it. Be quick about it too!"

Taking the bucket, I went to the alley, the concoction splashing inside like sludge against a river barge. Outside I quickly did what I was told to do and, when it was completed, carried the now almost-full container inside. I called to Mixer, who came to meet me in the hall and led me to a small closet, telling me to put a piece of cardboard on top of it to keep anything from falling into it and to leave it inside the closet for now.

Back in the main layout of the dive, he explained, "We got to wipe down the bar, the tables, then take out trash and tidy up. Then we go to the kitchen and fix it up for the bar food servin', and we get the hell out of Dodge. Before we go, we have to get our drink ready to take, so work with me, boy. Ain't got no time to waste!"

I knew enough to keep quiet, but as I looked around, I realized we could stay in this joint a month and not make it look any better—not unless we set it on fire! As for making the drink ready, my stomach turned with the thought! Me being me, I asked, "What about the cat?"

Mixer stopped a moment, then laughed harshly. "That damn cat can take care of his self and can hold its own liquor. Come on, boy, give me a hand with these bags!"

Getting bags, rinsing the barrels, and wiping things down went smoothly. During all this, that cat never moved from the position it had the first time I laid eyes on it. Mixer told me to gather bottles that had screw-on tops of various sizes and told me further to keep my sights out for pint and half-pints. He explained he had special customers. Really, "special customers"? I forced myself from imagining those special people and kept it moving.

Just as we were finishing the spot referred to as the kitchen, which was nothing but a small room with a stove, a refrigerator beside it, and a deep-stained sink and frying pans, the man that let us in came to speak to Mixer.

"Opening in 'bout an hour. You gonna be done?" he asked.

Mixer responded, "We be done before then."

"Here, I got to go for wings and things. Lock up," he said as he handed Mixer some bills.

When he left, Mixer turned to me and said, "Boy, go get our shit and bring those rags and stuff. We got to get!" I hurriedly went to retrieve our stash, bucket, bottles, rags, and newspaper and brought it all to the kitchen. Once I had it all there, I was told to get another bag and bucket. Off I went again. Coming back in this time, I saw Mixer slowly pouring the content into two large pots. He had the rags on top of the pots. Looking up at me, he said, "Come hold the rag so it don't fall in." I came near and held the sides of it to the pot as he poured a steady flow, screening, only pausing to allow the straining not to overflow. Once the two large pots were full, he beckoned me to move the empty bucket into position to continue the filtering. After the first filtering of the liquid, I was thoroughly sick of what I was seeing. However, we did this tree times, and each time the sludge became more and more fluid. My visceral response then was no less than what it was when we started, but I kept my upper lip stiff.

Mixer had gone from just a hobo filtering reconstituted liquor to a world-renowned chemist! Even in my repulsed state, I admired him.

With the last filtering done with a bar apron, he emphatically stated it was time to cook. I was taken aback by this, and it must have shown, because he said in his professional voice, "Boy, we got to heat it up to kill any nasty that's in it. But we can't do it fast, because it might blow."

Hearing that it might blow ended my being stupid. "What you mean *blow*?" I asked.

He looked at me like I had two heads, and said, "Damn, boy, we got 'nuff alcohol here to send us to hell and back, and now we got to heat it real careful."

He had my rapt attention now! He had me wipe down the outsides of the pots really good to ensure that none of the contents were on the side. It was a gas stove, and he turned the eyes on low flame and had me place the pots carefully on them. He got a long-handled wooden spoon and said metal could cause a spark. To tell you the truth, I don't know if anything he said was true, but right then and there, I believed him. I did stay away from the stove as the mad scientist was at work, and I stayed quiet and dumb! He had gone and retrieved two other empty five-gallon buckets and had me fill one halfway with ice. When he pronounced that the cooking was done, he rinsed the bar out and said we were to filter the contents from the pots into the five-gallon buckets. Pouring the ice in equal portions into both buckets, he had me pick the first part from the stove.

I asked, "Why?"

He said, "You're dumb but stronger than me, and your hand is more steady." He draped the apron over the bucket and added, "Start to pour real slow. The reason for the ice is to cool it so we can get it in the bottle, and the melted ice makes it drinkable with so many mixes in it."

That made perfect sense to me, but with my being stupid, you must consider what makes sense or not to a stupid person. He made sure that he stopped me pouring when the contents began to get to the bottom of the pots. Though we had screened and filtered, with this being the fourth time, there was still fine grit debris in the bottom. I was going to rinse the pots, but he stopped me and said what was in there was valuable. He mixed the contents together, placed it back on the stove, and brought it to a boil, then turned it off and put a lid on it. He turned to me and said, "Go get the cases of bottles we got stashed." I brought in both cartons, he found a funnel, and we began filling the bottles up to midneck. Mixer said to fill it any more could cause the bottles to burst from the gases. I didn't argue or question that rationale. We moved at a steady pace, and in no time our elixir was bottled. He took a much-larger-than-needed glass bottle and poured the warm contents into it and left the lid off. However, he did put a cloth stuffed into the opening to stop spillage.

"Come on, boy, we need to ghost out of here, fix up a little bit, and vamoose!"

We made quick work in covering our covert distilling and left out the door we came in, with Mixer setting the locks to lock when he closed the door. Just out of curiosity, I went to take a look at the cat, and yes, he was still there in the prone position, head at the awkward angle, with peanut and popcorn in its fur. There was one thing different, however: below the stool sat a small sardine can with our most recent product in it. Shaking my head going out, I thought to myself, *If he wasn't dead, he would be when he got into that batch!*

We loaded the wagon, carefully placing our booty securely. When all was to the satisfaction of Mixer, off we went. I did notice that with the weight inside the wagon, the squeaky wheels were a little quieter.

While we traveled up the street that we had come down on to get to the juke joint, Digger came hurriedly in the opposite direction. Seeing us, he broke into a smile and started waving a brown greasy bag in the air. Within speaking distance, he said, "Here, boy. Shoes said to give you this 'cause he knows that one there drinks his lunch." Giving me the bag, he looked expectantly at Mixer.

Mixer laughed a good laugh and, in response, said, "Well, I ain't the only lunch drinker, am I?" as he produced a small bottle with a grape-looking solution inside.

Digger took the proffered container in a smooth handoff and laughed. "Not by a long shot, you ole cooter!"

This got them both laughing till they started coughing and hacking. I knew this to be a worn-out line that they used all the time. I was too busy looking into the greasy bag to be concerned whether or not they'd die from laughing or coughing! Bacon, eggs, bread, home fries, and pastries were in it. All them mixed together didn't bother me, because it was all going the same way, anyway!

As we continued toward whatever the destination was, Digger walked and talked with Mixer. In between the rattling of the paper bag and chewing, I heard part of what was being talked about.

I'll give the narrative. Digger was explaining to Mixer that the plan for the week, and perhaps in the near future, was for all of us to stay at the mission for a few more days and let the rumble in the rail yard die down. All of us would then meet up at the meeting spot when Shoes gave the go-ahead, and the tribe would be discussing the business of winter coming, information relays from the West and South, and who would move and who would stay. As I listened to them, I was amazed yet again by the strategy and detailed plans of these people. I watched the town, active in life, and wondered if any of the "normal" ever thought that another society existed.

Digger left, and Mixer told me that we'd be stopping by one of the three auto shops where Fixer was doing cleanup and oil changes. As we were walking a little beyond the park, on the corner stood an old gas station. I had seen it yesterday, with the old rusted Esso sign on the marquee. Of course, we headed toward the back and came parallel with the back bays, and Fixer was dumping oil into a large drum.

"Hey, Fixer, I gotta drop off the mash. You know the plans?" called Mixer.

"Yeah. Shoes caught me before breakfast and told me. I got a spot. Come on."

We waited while he returned the bucket inside, and then he led us toward a small lean-to that had old tires and auto parts that appeared to have been there a long time. He moved various parts and tires, making a small space among the rusting debris, and bade us to unload our stock. After placing everything except several bottles into place, he began to blend our liquor stock into the trash head until nothing stood out of place. When he was satisfied with its concealment, he said, "There." As he walked up to us, I noticed a pronounced limp. He was a large Black man, with a ready smile, dressed in coveralls.

When he got close enough, Mixer handed him one of the fifths. "This here is the boy. Boy, this is Fixer."

He extended his hand and said, "Good to meet you." Then he asked, "So you the karate man, huh?"

"No, sir, just a man that don't like pain."

He winked at Mixer and replied, "Well, for a man that don't like pain, you sho 'nuff can dish it out!"

I said, "Have had my fair share on the receiving end and kind of figured out that giving it is a better end!"

That brought a roaring laugh from him, and in the quiet alley, it echoed like a foghorn! Mixer shook his head and was smiling and clapped me on the back, adding his approval. With that exchange, we heard a couple of cars pull up and signaled the dinging sound to let the gas attendant know of customers. Fixer said he had to get back and that before leaving he'd make sure the stash was more secure.

The rest of my day with Mixer revealed some of the inside secrets of tramping and the very thin line between road life and normal citizenship. I listened and asked questions. The day flew, and mission time naturally came; thus, the routine commenced.

The next couple of weeks were very busy for me. I was assigned to multiple individuals, and very rarely did they have a name. Almost in every instance, it was a monocle for what their trade was. Occasionally, only initials were used. The only name I can remember is Mary. I washed windows, mowed lawns, picked up trash, cleaned dog pens, and went to the dump outside of town. My days were so filled that I slept hard at night. All along, in the evenings, before sleep, Shoes would engage me about what I was learning and why I thought we were doing what we were doing and the specific reason for it. Digger, the constant class clown and antagonist, was there, adding his two cents and more! Each member that I was assigned with spoke of unity, preplanning, timing, and consistent effort of one and all. They took time to patiently explain the laws of cause and effect as it pertained to living alongside of and actually off society without becoming a parasite and draining them dry. The words *integrity* and *honor* stand out in my mind. This ragtag community not only contributed to their own but also looked for ways to help the standard social order. We even had eyes that watched the children and would-be predator alerts. Daily my astonishment grew, and the gratitude that I was adopted as well.

The days flowed and weeks came. About the third week, word filtered that the gathering would be next weekend and each faction was to have intel about their specific areas to share. Later, everyone would vote what would be the next move. I witnessed democracy! Democracy that rose from the ashes of rejection.

CHAPTER 15

The Hobo Summit

With the gathering date approaching, Shoes said I was going to be hanging with him. Although I enjoyed my time with each mentor, Shoes was really my favorite. As I reflect now, I realize I was the youngest member at thirty-three years old, and each one treated me as a younger brother, and the older ones as a son. Only Shoes would sometimes say my given name. Inheritably, I knew when he said my name that I'd better pay strict attention to what was going to be said. I couldn't begin to guess their ages; some looked ancient, and others youthful. Shoes looked both ways, if that was even possible. The entire community, both the real world and the displaced, considered him the leader. He never said that, and as a matter of fact, he just said he was nothing but a bum in the street. Yeah, in the street. But a bum? Most would agree. But having spent time with him, I think not!

Starting on Wednesday morning, once leaving the mission, we were in preparation for Saturday night at the rail yard. Until the gathering was over, all of us would be away from the mission, holed at night in various locations. Throughout Wednesday, Thursday, and Friday, Shoes and I traveled all over town and a few "outskirting" areas. He talked with individuals I had not met, spoke with shop owners and other common townsfolk. I knew to remain quiet and alert, so I stood a distance from his conversations. After each of them, though, he gave me a brief rundown and how it fit into the plans of the tribe. Several times he went to the police station, and three times to the post office. The last trip to the post office, he came out carrying a package. As usual, this did not surprise me; I had dwelled long enough with the tribe to know anything was possible, to the extent that if one of them landed a helicopter to deliver a pizza, I wouldn't have even blinked an eye!

He and I walked to the park with the package under his arm and sat on the bench. I scanned the park and felt the waning summer breeze and listened to the tearing of the paper as he began opening the package. By this time I had adapted enough not to be curious of its content. He started speaking as he inventoried what was on his lap. "Boy, you and me be skedaddling when the meet is over. Told you we'd be headed south before the first snow." He then continued, "Got the name Shoes 'cause I get some every few months. Most times, they be my size, sometimes somebody else's size."

Now, that drew my attention, so I looked squarely at him, then looked in the box, and then back at him. "These my size. I'm guessing your size too! About 10, wide!" He laughed. This was when the conversation took on another twist. "Listen, boy. If anything happens to me and you with me, you get my shoes and take my sidesaddle. I won't be needing them no more."

I had been in conversations before where I was aware that some things were being said and yet other things were not being said as well. This was one of those conversations, and even though I was a new hand to this outfit, I knew that this was monumental. "Shoes, exactly what you not telling me, and exactly what are you saying?" I asked.

Taking his time to form the answer, he, too, looked at the sky in its blueness and looked into the distance of the park, seeing and not seeing at the same time. Slowly, he said, "Michael, hear me good, son. Since day 1, I've tried to give what I've learned that has helped me. At no time did I hold secrets or judge who and what you are. You're a good boy, and only God knows what put you on the road, but on the road you are. To live this, you need real understanding, not that jack-shit schooling, but real-time, applied shit, for the here and now! Now, you remember what I told you about how your feet will make you or break you?"

I nodded my assent.

"Well, when two or three of us walk together, the unspoken rule is that if one dies, the others share what has been left behind to continue to live. Consider it an inheritance, just like normal people do with their money, property, etc."

"Shoes, this ain't like 'normal people' shit you talking about now!" I exclaimed.

He said, "None of this ain't normal, boy! Therefore, shut up and listen to this, for your own good. You got to live, boy. You got to keep walking where you got to go. Maybe one damn day you'll be able to walk off this fucking road and live to tell about it."

Shoes had never talked that harshly to me before this moment. I knew in my heart of hearts that this was important to him, that I understood this unspoken word. "You got an obligation here," he said. "And that obligation is to yourself and to others. So I am telling you to take my shoes, take my sidesaddle, and live, because everything I got is useful to you. It won't do a damn thing in the hereafter! I've been giving people shoes since I been on the road. I been doing it because it's all I can do for them, any of them, in the hopes that they find their way. You got a chance. Now, I really don't want to sit here and talk about what should be obvious. It's quite possible Digger's right: your mama might not have had any children that lived!" He chuckled at his own quote from Digger. I laughed too (to put him at ease and for my immeasurable respect for him) and told him that I would do what he said. However, deep inside of me, I could not imagine that I could ever do that "grave robbing." Thinking about it, I realized it really wouldn't be grave robbing, because he wasn't buried in the ground or in a tomb. Yet the very idea sounded a lot like it was from the same ballpark, because in my fiber I felt like, as a human being, it was desecration of the dead! Yet for the past month, I had been in the custodial care of an amazing people, with Shoes representing the messiah.

Throughout the rest of the day, we continued to make our rounds, and Shoes continued with his brief, and sometimes long, conferences with individuals and small groupings. I stood aside within listening distance and yet heard very little because of the silence incubated within my own thoughts.

As members of a tribe, each member went about their assigned affairs with purpose. Each of us knew that the appointed gathering would yield information that was assimilated and placed into a workable pursuit of survival. For me, it was a time of a blur of activity, somewhat disjointed in the measurement of time. This might be attributed to my being new to the scene of hoboism or simply that of a neophyte. Whatever the reason, I cannot recount in very much detail all the activities of those several days. What I am most positive about is that a feeling of foreboding accompanied me. However, it wasn't the same as a feeling of doom. Yes, I constantly attempted to discern it, but in every turn, I could not grasp its true meaning. Never once did I give up on trying, but never could I shed an internal light on exactly what it was. Shoes continued his lessons, during the day and in the evenings, in our makeshift lodgings, prior to gathering night. It wasn't until later, after this entire chapter had ended and on our parting on the road, that the topics and lessons took hold. It is in these memories and epiphanies of later that I have come to know that there are wise men among us and that in every section and subsection of our world, there are beacons assigned so that light, hope, and direction remain available to all within our masses.

Gathering outside of the town limits within the wooded area of the hillside, the people came. They came in twos, threes, and small groupings throughout Saturday. Shoes, Digger, Mary, and I got there early after sunrise. Mary and I were told to find branches and such to make and feed the fires for the night. Needless to say, I was somewhat concerned to have to work with Mary and her bat in close proximity. I did what was asked of me, however, and lifted a small prayer to heaven that I didn't come back to base camp with raised knots on my head! But what I found surprised me. Mary was a great conversationalist and quite pleasant. At times she was humorous. I will say this: I still ensured keeping my distance and only spoke when spoken to or when there was need to answer or ask questions. Multiple trips to and from the forest were made, and each time upon our return, more people showed up. Quick breaks and long workings transformed an isolated location into a community of tents, makeshift lean-tos, and patches of plotted dwellings. I saw how out of nothingness came life and purpose. I witnessed camaraderie of people, race, gender, religion, old, young, and a mixture of purity, which I had seldom seen. Stirring within me was a shout that I was home! I was confused and yet comforted as well. It was as if all these strangers were family or relatives that had not seen one another in some time. There were conversations in gaiety, sometimes sad reminiscing, but in all these, there was the spirit of community! The emotions and feelings of safety in numbers and love enfolded all of us. Finally, our journeys were over, and we were home.

As dusk began to fall and the settling had given way to small instruments of guitars, fiddles, harmonicas, wooden flutes, Gizoos, and makeshift drums of five-gallon buckets, facedown, and yes, several renditions sang of the anthem "Wretch Song." Various fires were lit, announcing the beginning of the gathering conferences.

Shoes said that he'd be busy and told me that I was to stay with Mary in a certain section and do what she told me to do. He must have noticed my obvious fear of her bat, for he said, "Don't worry, boy, she has taken a liking to you and feels that you are special to me." He said this with a smile. And with that being said, I felt a hand placed on my shoulder and turned. It was Mary, One Eye, with a gentle smile, saying, "Come on, son. We're going to sit here." Wonders never cease! For the first time since our introduction at the lunch hall, I felt real warmth from her. Then she added, "I still got my bat!" Smiling, I obediently followed her one-eyed lead to our spot and then sat, thinking to myself that I was in the safest place sitting beside her.

A bugle sounded, and a hush fell upon the grouping. Shoes stepped onto the raised mound, makeshift platform constructed by Fixer and a half-dozen others throughout the day. Looking about him, he began, "Welcome, family, and I thank all of you for coming. There is much to discuss here, and we must get it done. The future depends on how we conduct ourselves tonight and from henceforth. Our ways are becoming lost to those that now are coming on the road, and we of the older breed are dying out. Much is happening in the world as we know it. Much will be changing, and with the change about us, so too must we change or we, as a whole, will die!"

That was a very ominous term, even for my untrained ears. I knew something was about to change and that whatever it was would affect not only this grouping but also the entire world. How I knew that what he was speaking of and would be covered throughout this night was true, I can't explain, nor will I try to even give an explanation now. I ask you, the reader, to merely accept what I did and move along. However, in an attempt to allay any misgivings that any may have about accepting this surmising, I will state this simple fact: During the rest of my ensuing years on the road, much of what Shoes covered in that dialogue in the woods, to the ears of a disjointed and separated people, had come to pass within our world. I am speaking not only of the homeless world but also of the world as in the planet Earth.

One by one he called each group from whatever area they came from toward the platform and spoke directly with them. Much of the conversations, I could not hear or understand. Throughout the encampment, as if prearranged, factions assembled and conversed among themselves before their group was called before their messiah. I observed both, in listening and feeling. The evening was warm, not hot, and the summer breeze gave way to the waves of cooling air of the fall.

Mary nudged me and said, "Come on, boy." She got up and started toward the tree line, warning me to watch my step. Surprisingly, we passed multiple assigned sentries of sorts, some in bushes, others up in the trees. I looked about with new interest at the organization and security of these harmless individuals. Soon I began to question myself whether or not they were truly harmless. I ended this conference with the fact that they were self-preserving! Traveling a short distance from our gathering, Mary and I came to a small pathway. It appeared to be an animal trail, and standing there, to my surprise, was the ape-man (a.k.a. the pecker checker). Mary went to him, and they embraced. This solved the mystery of how she was able to get into the men's mission at night. He had with him a small lamp, the kerosene type, and a blanket, in which he wrapped around the shoulders of his woman. He looked at me and said, "Now you know." He said this as if he knew that I was trying to solve a constantly changing puzzle, so he just presented one of the pieces.

Breaking my dream state, Mary said, "Let's be heading back," as she took his paw into her hand, just like a schoolgirl.

As we walked back, I fell into step a little behind out of respect and since Shoes had taught me never to walk three abreast, because three across blocked foot traffic in both directions and it was disrespect to another traveler. Mary said his name, but I can't remember it, for I was caught in yet another surprise. She spoke lovingly of how he used to be a pro wrestler of some sort and had fallen from grace. This explained his massive size and his function to the tribe and its needs. At every twist and turn, almost daily since my falling into this rabbit hole, I became aware of just how many things I truly didn't know!

While we made our way past the hidden sentries, the pecker checker would stop at some of the sentries and greet them and hand out a small package, its content I couldn't see. Sometimes it was a small bottle that I could see! Back into the common area, we took our places. Soon we were joined with individuals that I had become familiar with, and they began talking of our district. Yes, I say *district*, and I came up with this because, by all my practical observing, the groupings did represent districts.

While Digger, Mixer, Fixer, Ape-Man, and others talked, Mary leaned into me and said, "Michael, you going to be going with Shoes when this is over? Whatever he tells you will be true, true. He's like Moses to these people, and I love him. For years that I have known him, he hasn't said much about himself, and less about where he's been. Now, you know the rule: it ain't nobody's business but your own, until you choose to let it be known. That's how it's been between us. He's a real man. He's got a heart of gold, but I think that he carries a heavy cross on him. It doesn't weigh him to the point that he doesn't think of others. Instead, it drives him to make sure that our people are safe, or at least as safe as this type of life can get. I told you, he is Moses, as sure as I'm sitting here and as sure as you are sitting there!"

I went to interrupt, but she threatened that if I should say one thing before she was done, she'd hit me with that fool bat! I clammed real quickly at her intense stare and rushed speech to get it all out before any took notice. As she stared at me with her sighted eye, it was as though I was watching her soul speak.

"I love him," she continued, "not like a woman and a man, but like a brother, father, uncle, and everything that is good and pure. He gave all of us himself, and in return, we became alive! We became a people, though not like society, and I ain't saying society failed us or that we failed society, though the commoners think that we did. They say we couldn't cut the mustard, and the fact is, most of us believed that too. Shoes showed us that, in fact, we could cut the mustard but instead we were called out. He's Moses, and you are his Aaron! Make sure you do what he says. I suppose this will be the last time that I'll be seeing my friend at one of these. Boy, this is Egypt land, if it ever was one at all, and all of us are headed to the Red Sea!"

I remember that one-sided conversation to this day. As I sit rehashing it into the writing before your eyes, I can smell and hear the encampment. The music and feel, the atmosphere of celebration. Not all the happenings are still clear to me, for many years have passed since those days of relearning, but I do recall that most of my inner dialogue was something of this nature. Egypt and the Nile River are not in the good ole USA, and I'm quite certain that Shoes was not pulled from a river's edge and raised by a pharaoh's daughter! I was by no means an Aaron, and any stick that I would pick up would always be nothing but a stick, not a serpent that ate other snakes! Yet even with this rationale, a shiver on that warm night ran through my body. Much of the great gathering is not remembered; I suspect that what Mary had told me kept me occupied.

Finally, our core group was called, and as we approached, Shoes looked at me and said, "You and I will talk later. Go to the woods and start relieving those that watch, so they can eat, rest, drink, and see some of their people."

I turned without question for sentry duty. It was good that I would have some time to myself. As I think back on it, I realize it never entered my mind why I was designated to be the relief; it just felt as natural as rain to do my part.

This ends the basics of the gathering. The night bled into the early dawning of the next day. Music, food, drink, fellowship, and most of all, the atmosphere of unity are what I remember best. The visitors began packing and cleaning. All firepits, which were well attended the night before, were now being filled in, and the earth smoothed over. The exodus began in quietly filtering droves. Disappearing as they had come, the tribes or communities returned to their areas.

By Sunday at dusk, it appeared as if nothing had ever happened. We of our community were once again just a few homeless, harmless, down-and-out men and women. However, I had witnessed an unexplainable phenomenon: I had participated in an awakening that few would have. I was no longer apart from but a part of! I was a hobo!

CHAPTER 16 ──────────────────────

Two for the Road

Our community was purpose driven over the next few days. Routine assignments of window washings, lawn services, information gathering, and the run-of-the-mill stuff had a sense of urgency. One could feel the vibratory aftermath of what I would call the summit. I could feel this vibration, but I kept the feeling to myself, attributing it to my recent experience of the "hobo baptism." What was most apparent is that I was being outfitted for the soon-to-be road trip that Shoes and I were going to be taking. I really can't recall very many details in this preparation, but I do know that I was kept busy and the elders would speak to me of many of their experiences and how the lessons learned had enabled them to continue to live. As for Shoes, we spent much of the time apart while I was assigned to others. During the evening, we had taken to alternating our places of refuge between the rail yards, the mission, and the surrounding wooded area. Once, I did ask about the change of venue for the gathering and was told by someone that it had been changed because the size of the crowd would have drawn attention. There was no further discussion on the subject, nor did it come up about the information received and dispatched to each tribe.

The day finally arrived. The previous night, while we were in the mission, during our In between the Bunk Conference, Shoes spoke with me, Digger, and a few others, saying that tomorrow he and I would be headed out. I listened, but I did not hear, because my mind was full of expectations of what would come. However, I do remember fragments of it.

"Digger, you know what to do. Keep watch on those developments, and if anything changes, get word to me or send word up north."

Long after lights were out, the men continued. I was awakened by the jarring of the bunk and Digger loudly saying, "Daylight is wasting. Get up, boy!" In all my imaginings, I would never have imagined that I'd be lulled to sleep by the intense murmurings of a bunch of misfits! Yet that was exactly what had happened. Hurriedly, I gathered my possessions. All of us went to the feeding hall and then exited the building. Digger, Shoes, Fixer, and I walked the now-familiar street, and it didn't cease to amaze me watching the town wake up from sleep and go about its day.

While walking in what I assumed to be south, we were joined by one or two. By the time we reached the town's city limits, we had a small but noticeable crowd parading. Mary, Ape-Man, Mixer, and a host of others met us in farewell. Some were talking among themselves, and others butting into private conversations and joking and smack talking. I knew I could feel the longing sorrow of the goodbye that was to come.

Finally, Shoes spoke and the assembly quieted. "Me and the boy are headed out. All of you know what to do. It's important that we take care of one another and that we take care of the place we stay in. This makes no matter how they think of us. It only matters how we think of ourselves. I'll probably see you in late spring or midsummer. I might head out west, though, so it may be as late as fall." He turned to me. "Come on, boy, we got to get."

Mary, with one eye crying, hugged Shoes, and ole Digger pulled out a fresh pint glass bottle and handed it to Shoes, saying, "I'd give it to the boy, but he'd probably bust the glass. You know, he don't know shit yet!" He then winked at me and shook my hand. Shoes led the way, and I followed a half-step behind. I felt sad and a small apprehension at leaving these people. Though I was with a leader, I still felt alone, not like the womb of community that I had grown accustomed to. Shoes, as if reading my thoughts, said, "Son, on the road, there will be many goodbyes and a few happy reunions. You got to remember this. This is the page we choose, and on this page are many things. However, out of the many things we will only learn a few."

That commentary brought with it a shadow of foreboding. Before I could try to wrap my mind around it to understand, he went on, "So we enjoy the moments of joy. We treat one another with respect. We try to help, not just our own, but any who is in need as well. We learn to love our depravity and our freedom, and by God, we stand for all that is good and decent. It is when a person tries to live like this to the best of their ability that when the time comes to lay to rest, we won't be afraid of what's in the hereafter."

Everything that he had said before that had caused me distress was erased, because in his speaking, this was the direction of right living, and it could heal the sadness in parting ways with those that you cared for and loved. I realized that I had come to love these strange people and cared for them. I do not know when this happened, but what Shoes said stirred my inners and the stone-cold truth emerged. Not long after this, as we continued our trek, a semi rolled up to us and gave us a lift. I wouldn't have been surprised if the driver didn't know Shoes, but we rode in silence in the back of the truck, each to his own thoughts.

I was awakened later by the slowing down of the truck, the sharp turning, and the air brakes being applied. I looked about me in the dim light in the back, and Shoes said, "We covered a good piece for one today. We'll rest up here and head out tomorrow. We covered about seventy-five miles."

Gathering our stuff and climbing from the back, I saw we were at one of those interstate truck stops. Shoes went to the cab and spoke with the driver for a few moments, then returned to me. "Let's go do some checking," he said. We entered a small mall-like building; it had a convenience store, restaurant, small arcade, phone booths, and restrooms. I was fascinated because I hadn't ever seen anything like this. In the back of a trucker motel and a bunkhouse for showers and back on the road quick rest stops.

Ogling, Shoes said, "Michael, you got to blend in and look like you belong, so put your tongue back in your mouth, quit looking around like a kid in a candy store, and for goodness' sake, stop walking like that!"

Walking like what? I wondered.

No sooner had he said it than I realized that, indeed, I was walking like an individual that was mentally and physically challenged. How in the hell did that transformation creep up on me? I can't explain it, and I am quite certain that maybe psychology would have an apt term for that! I got a grip on myself and, embarrassed, followed him to the shower area.

There, he spoke with the attendant, handed some cash over, and told me to follow him. We went down a hallway and entered a room with the single beds in it; at the foot of each bed was a footlocker. I selected my bunk, and Shoes took the one closest to me. "Before we shower and bunk down, let's get some food and snacks for tomorrow," he said.

When we entered the mall again, I saw that there just wasn't one restaurant but several. He led us to a buffet. "Always select buffets. Go straight to the meats, the vegetables then, and worry about desserts last. Always get as much protein as you can get. Vegetables are a powerhouse. They give you a variety of different vitamins and help keep your bowels regular. Listen, you got to keep yourself regular. What goes in got to come out. It can't stay up in you too long, or it will turn your insides bad, and then you got real trouble. Boy, you got to pay attention to what you eating and how often you eating it. If you living on the road, meat, fat, and all sorts of things in meat will give you the extra 'oomph' to make it to your next. Only a fool will run to desserts—they are full of nothing and will kill you quicker than anything. Believe it or not, it's good not to eat every day. If you're drinking water, not those bullshit drinks, but honest-to-God water, that'll do you better than anything. So when it's time to eat, your body is ready and goes at digesting it."

After the lecture, he turned and we entered the buffet. I imitated every food selection he did, even the slimy boiled okra! We ate and ate some more. We ate till full, and then Shoes demonstrated the art of food smuggling.

Shoes showed me what I called hush puppies. He called them corn pone. He said that you'd always want to get at least six to a half-dozen, that you could store them in your sidesaddle, sometimes up to six months. I was amazed because, he said, when you added water or any liquid to them, in a pinch you wouldn't starve. I was reminded to always keep plastic bread wrappers with me, because anything from liquids to full-course meals could be pilfered out inside of a pant leg or underwear. He reminded me that briefs, as opposed to boxers, are best in food runs. Depending on what commodity I'd be trying to liberate, perhaps a pair of long johns might be beneficial.

He brought me to tears once with the tale of one hunchback booster. It went something like this.

This guy did have a hunch in his back; however, his specialty was that he always made the hunch look larger than it actually was. He did this by stuffing items, such as clothing, under his shirts or the coats that he wore. Whenever he'd come across an item or items to be taken, the only thing that he would do was remove some of the padding covering the hunch and go about his business. After so long at this gaffing, he became quite good. For the longest time, he never got caught and was never bothered. One day he went in a small mom-and-pop store, and of course, there were items begging to be taken. So being the thief that he was, he did what he did best. Leaving the store, he walked to the corner and there stood the owner with a shotgun pointed at him. Of course, the hunchback inquired what the problem was, and the shop owner explained that the merchandise on his hump needed to be paid for. Of course, the thief denied any such thing. At gunpoint, the shop owner led this crippled villain back to the scene of the crime. Upon arriving at the scene of the crime, the shop owner and the hunchback were met by the shop owner's daughter. She told the hunchback to hand over the merchandise and be on his way. Strangely enough, he did, and as he was wiggling the ill-gotten gains from his back, he asked the shopkeeper's daughter if she would go out with him.

I looked at Shoes, and he said, "Wasn't too long after that that they got married."

"What!" I said.

"Yeah. She was a hunchback too!" He howled with laughter.

That was the most stupid thing that I had heard in a long time, and what was funny was that I was so enthralled with the story that he just kept weaving it! Important things sometimes I can't remember, but something like this stupid tale, I can. Sometimes, fact is stranger than fiction. What is more of a fact is that this was the first time, in my recollection, that I had heard Shoes tell anything resembling a joke. As a matter of fact, once he and I started our journey, I noticed something about his demeanor as we traveled farther from our diggings. I think I may have to chalk his change up to sadness in leaving his begotten family, so naturally I thought it would pass. It did pass, but not in the way I thought it would.

The night passed peacefully, and early in the morning, we took once again to the road. Once we were outside of the small mall-like structure, Shoes said, "Son, we're going to foot-travel today. I know some of these parts and got a few spots that we'll be able to hunker for this evening."

We walked in silence toward the interstate, but before actually getting to the highway, we turned toward a small route road. This was lined with trees and wooded areas. The day had all the telltale signs of the approaching autumn season and yet still held the warmth of late summer. I can say that it was comfortable. Looking through the thinning trees, I could see tobacco sheds, farmhouses, and even one or two bunkhouses, which Shoes pointed out. As I was a city boy, it never stopped to amaze me seeing wildlife up close. Indeed, squirrels, rabbits, and an occasional raccoon, but deer, and groundhogs scurrying across the road, these were my constant delight. In the afternoon, he called a rest, and we made our way closer to the tree line, just in case maybe the country sheriff department might be doing patrols. While looking for the right spot, I heard, more so than seen, the nesting site for some forest animal. It sounded like kittens to me, and so I started to follow the sound. Sure enough, as fortune would have it, I found what was making the sounds, a litter of tiny creatures. I couldn't identify them by sight, but they were very cute.

I called to Shoes to come look at this. He made his way toward me, and when he got to me, he stood stock-still and placed a guarded hand on my right upper arm. "Look here, boy. We 'bout to be in a whole lot of mess! Stay still, don't breathe, and don't do anything!" He said this through clenched teeth and in a hushed whisper both at the same time, if possible. I went to say something, but he quickly put his finger to his lips, demanding immediate silence. Still confused at what had alarmed him so, I heard the bushes to my right start to shake, and a hissing sound, not like a snake's, but like that of a cat, caught my attention. Shoes began to ease back while he held steady, pulling tension on my arm for me to backtrack with him. Then, through the brush came two large skunks. Shoes let go of my arm and yelled, "Run!"

Back in the day, I was fast; however, that day, Shoes was Flash Gordon!

While we were picking them up and putting them down, the skunks were in hot pursuit. Between the uneven surface and the brambles and low-hanging branches, our pursuers appeared to be gaining. At least gaining on me, because I had lost sight of Shoes! The only thing I can tell you for certain is that I felt some moisture hit from behind and felt a spraying on my left leg, but you can be certain I didn't break stride until I heard Shoes calling me from a distance behind me. Somehow he had cut to the side and I had passed him in my haste. I stopped and started looking around for my attackers. I didn't see them. I called out to Shoes, and he called back to me. It was like we were using sonar to get to each other. Finally coming to a less-dense spot among the trees, I saw Shoes sitting on a fallen tree, taking his shoes off. Looking at me, he burst into laughter. I had brambles up and down my pant legs, my glasses were askew, I had ripped my jacket, leaves and underbrush were in my nappy hair, and I had been skunked!

He put his hands up and said, "You stay right there. Yo skunked, and we got a mess on our hands!"

I had always thought that the smell of a skunk would be putrid, something like the smell of runny stool. Skunk smell is putrid, all right, but it's smell that is like none other! Not only do you smell bad, but something about it also affects your eyes! My eyes were burning and tearing like crazy, my nose was running, and when the wind shifted to blow back on me, the smell had me gagging.

Shoes said that we couldn't continue for the day because we had to deal with this right now. He led me to a stream nearby, and I had to strip and get into the cold water. He had me take the sandy or gritty soil within the streambed to scrub myself over and over. My clothes were also submerged into the stream, held down with heavy rocks. Starting a fire, he didn't allow me to get into any clean clothing because of the recent skunking but had me sit in the sun near the fire. To help take the matter in stride, he handed me Digger's elixir to gulp, to help with warmth. I was a miserable cuss; in the woods, near a fire, butt-ball naked, with a hobo who would occasionally look at me in my forlorn state and burst into tear-streaming gales of laughter was not my idea of fun! After several more dips and scrubs in the streambed, Shoes pronounced that that was all we could do for now.

"We're going to build a lean-to for this night's camp. After we got it together, I'm going to head out and get some stuff to help clear you up. We got a distance still to go, but ain't nobody willing to put up with a skunk, so we got to get this as tight as possible," he said. Afterward, he sent me scavenging for twigs, boughs, thin sticks, and branches with leaves still in them. Forty-five minutes to an hour later, we had accommodations for the soon-approaching night.

"Look, I know a few peoples in this area. I'll be back by night-fall. You going to be okay?"

Shoes had given me the pants and shirt he had on to wear while my skunked garments hung on some bushes downwind from camp. He dressed in his second set. I nodded that all would be fine, and with that, he set out on his "deskunking" mission.

The woods were quiet, the breeze warm and gentle. I was used to the quiet and did enjoy the company of myself. I recounted, the past two to three months, it might have been longer. You see, after a while on the road, you would notice time no longer existed as it once had, by calendar or by clock; instead, time was measured in events, the sweeping hand of the clock becoming movement in living color of all our activities for survival. I, once again, cannot pinpoint when this type of perception began, but its coming into being was just a naturally growing thing since my introduction into the hobo life.

Before Shoes left, he discussed briefly our crude alarm system setup. It went something like this: Returning to the camp, and to ensure that I knew it was him, he would begin to clap two stones together. These stones would be large enough to withstand hard clapping together without breaking and to cause a loud-enough sound, not to be confused with the normal forest sound. We went to the stream and searched for some stones and tested his system by the streambed. Shoes explained that if we could hear the clapping over the sound of the stream, it would certainly be loud enough to distinguish at our campsite. He would start clapping a series of patterns that we agreed to be at one-minute increments. I was to stay alert after dark and keep the fire stoked enough that once I heard and responded, it was to make sure that the fire could be visible by him. In addition, Shoes further explained that others knew of coded messaging, so I was to note the rhythm carefully, because it was possible that responding to fakery could be fatal. We practiced our coding several more times, until I felt confident with identifying the rhythm.

"Boy, when the coding starts, move all items of worth toward the opposite direction from where you hear the sound. Make sure that you gauge the distance and keep to the shadows, even though you stoke up the fire. This will give you an advantage with the fire in their eyes, just in case they have no good intentions."

Hearing this did not alarm me or cause me fear. I was amazed at the depth and quality of the skills that he shared with me.

Going back to the site, he turned and looked at me, smiling. "Boy, it's been a while since I've had a tenderfoot on the trail with me, and I damn sho don't miss it!" Shoes said. "Shit, running like hell in the woods and getting skunked!" He couldn't finish because laughter took over until he had a hacking, coughing bout. After he had gotten himself under control again, though a hint of hilarity threatened his attempt to command, he told me to get some of the sand from the stream and spread and dry them in the sun. He explained that I should continue to rub it on my affected areas and it would simmer down the smell over time. I was also to do my feet, being that we'd be hold up here at least for another day and that now was the time because once we hit the road again, we'd be traveling to get to our stopping point.

I watched him fade into the density of the trees and sat listening to the sounds of nature. On occasion, I would look into the clear sky and watch cloud formations, with the dusting of flocks of birds. Finally, I hefted myself from daydreaming and headed toward the streambed to retrieve some of the bottom sandy soil to dry, as instructed by Shoes. I found a large piece of tree bark that was strong enough to support the weight and large enough that I wouldn't have to make multiple trips. Done with the task of spreading it to dry, I set about doing my ritual of feet care. Sometimes, with the changing direction of the wind, I'd get a whiff of skunk while doing my feet. I found a small piece of sandstone and filed at my toenails. While I did these mundane but important tasks, my mind recounted the events that had ensued.

I began to think on the summer day in June of 1975, when I was moving from my parents' for the first time. My girlfriend had become pregnant, and I decided I was going to do the right thing and marry her so that the child wouldn't be a bastard. At the age of eighteen, with no clue of what I wanted to do or how I would support a family, I announced my manly intent. To marry, take care of my responsibility, and make everyone proud. Remembering this, I smiled to myself. The scene continued to play within my mind's eye. I was moving boxes this time. I had convinced an older friend who owned a home to allow me to come and build a small apartment in his basement for myself and my would-be bride. So with a sense of purpose and at least a direction to follow, I packed my childhood into boxes and shouldered what I thought to be manhood! Cramming and pushing all types of items into the waiting Volkswagen minivan, I turned to see my mom watching me. Almost done with the tasks at hand, I went to where she stood and asked in my newfound manhood if she was okay. She extended her hand and placed it gently on my right shoulder. "Michael, what are you going to do?" she asked.

In the seventies, just like in all eras of people becoming hip, slick, or cool, there was a saying: "I'm going to find myself." And that was what I said.

Mom looked at me with a glinting twinkle in her eye. "Son," she said, "you are going to find that when you find yourself, you were with you all the time."

I didn't feel deflated at that time; she was careful not to deflate my fragile, new manhood. What she told me next, though, was something I have never forgotten and, at times, when all chips had been down and were not in my favor, I recalled what Mom said on that June day of my departure. "Life is like a dragon," she began. "There are only three positions: One, you grab onto its tail and be dragged wherever it chooses to go. The second spot—and most people think this is a good spot, but it's really not—is to hop onto its back and ride like you would a horse or beast of burden. However, dragons are large, and the very size makes it unruly and difficult to tame, because it is not a beast of burden. It is the essence of all that we are! Michael, the dragon is life, and it has been here all the time. You, my son, are the only thing passing through! So that is not the best position for you! To find yourself, as you say that you are going to do, you must battle this beast, and you must get it in a headlock, just like wrestlers do. With it under your arm, as you apply the pressure and the direction, you have a mighty beast at your disposal! This is by no means an easy thing. Many have tried, and few have succeeded! Son, most believe it's about power through money and strength and control. Indeed, some of these come with harnessing the dragon. However, there are greater things than trying to rule man or having the last say-so."

My mom had never spoken to me in such a metaphor before. And so I didn't realize that this conversation was a rite of passage, an acknowledgment that her baby, her son, her child, was now accepted as a man. Though she did not agree on the subject of marriage, she would not interfere with decisions that I alone should make. She hugged me, and though I knew it wasn't like farewell, I know now today that what passed between us were the severing rites of the apron strings from my mom. Yes, that was one of the very first "one of many" moments that forged the next coming moment, bringing us closer to a certain mystery of a truth. Tears fell. I missed my mom. I missed the moments that I didn't spend in honor of her. I am thankful to have memory and the cut of pained remorse, reminding me not to repeat actions that harm.

Shaking myself from my reverie, I knew that there were things that needed to be done while I waited for Shoes's return. I went to gather more kindling, wood, and fire-starting material for a long, slow burn. Going into the surrounding area, I gathered foodstuff—berries, pecans, wild onions, and turnips—for a meager meal. I rubbed the sandy soil on me and removed my clothing to allow more airing and rewashed my clothing that had been skunked, spreading them on bushes in the sun. Remembering what Shoes had said about signaling, I ensured which locations would be best to shadow in that night. Once these chores were done, and the meager rationing set up, I decided it was best to nap awhile, because there was no telling just how late his return might be. The sun was beyond the afternoon height, and I lay in the lean-to with my pack under my head and my shoes on. I slept peacefully and, awakening later, found that I had slept into the dusk of day. Feeling refreshed, I rekindled the fire and slow-stoked it, to have not a large flame but a low burn. I moved all my pieces into place and used the coming darkness to select exit points and places of concealment. I remembered not to look directly into the flame to keep my night vision as good as possible.

It was quiet in the evening, and occasionally, with the rising of the moon of the night, I could see and hear deer wandering and see bushes rattling with undergrowth night life. Surprisingly, this was not a fearful time. I was part of this natural time. It was comforting to know and feel the natural flow. It was at an interval of slow stoking that I could hear off in the distance the triple clacking of stones. I waited, and about a minute later came the same prearranged clacking sound. Certain now that I had heard, I responded. Just as Shoes had told me, I moved to the shadows and kept to them. Moments later, and this time closer than before, the signal sounded again. Again, keeping to the shadows, I responded. This Morse code of sorts continued for fifteen minutes before a shadowy figured stepped into the small glow of the encampment. Walking toward the fire to be identified, Shoes gently called me by name. I ghosted in from the shadows.

I could see that the journey had taken a toll on him. He looked tired. I let him know that I had made a stew out of some of the things we had and what I had found. That it was warm because I kept the cooking cans on rocks by the fire so that he could eat when he got back. He told me briefly of his trip, about thirty miles in all. He caught rides and legged to a small town, met up with tribes of people, and was directed to other places. And it had been profitable. He got some vinegar, tomato juice, baking soda, and some moonshine and some edibles, because we were getting low. He said he was tuckered out; he would eat some of the stew and go to sleep.

I was concerned and felt to blame because I was the cause of the skunking, but I said nothing. I watched him eat quietly, and then taking the moonshine and the remnants of Mixer's elixir, he mixed them together and shook the container. He said, "We'll take a couple of slugs apiece and we'll sleep fine."

And that was what we did, said our "Good nights," and I was dead to the world.

Just like that.

CHAPTER 17 ———————————

Off to See the Widow

I awoke to an overcast morning and some type of insect exploring my neck. Quickly brushing the unexpected interloper aside, I sat up. Looking about me, I saw that the fire had died down during the course of the night. More astonishing was that Shoes still was asleep, curled in a fetal position, facing where the warm fire had been. Attempting to be as quiet as possible to allow him more rest, I decided to do my foot routine before the start of our day.

While undoing them, I carefully watched the rise and fall of the sleeping form. Being able to really see him, I saw his resting state and the toll that road life had taken on him. Another thing that I noticed, I could not describe at the time, but later in this discourse I will. Removing shoes and socks and setting them aside, I began my inspection of each and the necessary ministrations, as I had been taught. I do recall the strange gut feelings that stirred in me as I watched Shoes's sleeping body. In all the time of our being together, I could not recall an instance that he was not up and about, no matter what time I came into consciousness. After the ritual of my feet, I went about the tasks of making the fire, gathering fresh drinking water, and also brought enough so that Shoes would have enough to bird-bathe when he awakened.

Not too long after I set things into motion, he began to stir. I had already gathered some of the late-season berries I could fire around and put the coffee on. Our coffeepot was actually a sock full of ground beans that we would place into a can of water and let simmer on a rock in the fire.

Rubbing his face vigorously and scratching at his head, he sat up and ushered out a "Good morning." I felt my uneasiness abate somewhat as I watched him begin the ritual that he had taught me. Moving about, not to show any of my secret concern, I prepared the meager breakfast and coffee and set it within his arm's length, which he thanked me for. In silence he ate, and I emptied my sidesaddle of its contents to begin inventory. Shoes looked around and continued to consume our whatnot breakfast and spoke out. "Fit for a king, my boy!" he said. Looking up from my labor, I saw him holding up one of the wild berries I had gathered, and I smiled at him.

I moved on from my saddlebag, reordering its contents, and started camp pickup. I was taught that camp pickup was necessary; this kept the woods clean and helped prevent fires or cause any close scrutiny from the surrounding community in regards to tramps too close for comfort. Shoes went about his affairs, assured that all that needed to be done was being done properly. This gave me a feeling of personal accomplishment that I could do such an important task without direction. However, though my misgivings about his health had abated somewhat, it still niggled my insides that perhaps he was feeling worse than he let on. I continued to beat myself about being skunked and his having to take on the extra burden of traveling and returning for my sake. Never did he mumble a word about where he went, how he had traveled, and whom he had to see, and neither did I ask.

Around noon, while we sat, Shoes spoke again. "Son, we got a bit of woods traveling today, maybe seven to ten miles. These are going to be real country miles, because we're going to be traveling the woods. Don't worry, it won't be hard, just a lot of walking trails."

I asked, "Which direction?"

"Southwest," he said, "but there'll be a lot of cutbacks, so you'll probably lose your sense of direction."

Close to half an hour later, after ensuring our campsite was in order, we headed in a southern direction following a small animal trail. During this leisurely pace, Shoes spoke casually about all that

I had been exposed to since coming under his supervision. He questioned me on different tactics of road life and answered patiently any questions I had. After two hours of path walking and class recitation, he called for a rest. We had stayed close to the banks of the stream, so we headed closer to the shore. Going toward it, he told me to watch for animal tracks, though he couldn't identify all tracks. He said, "What you really look for this deep in the woods are bear and cat tracks. These are easier to know. When you see these, be careful, because they need to drink as well. They're very territorial and will attack. You already know that skunks will protect their young!"

Laughing, I said, "Don't I know it!"

After chuckling, he added, "The good thing about being skunked is, most animals can smell it and pretty much keep away from you, but bears and cats may be more hungry than be put off by stink, so make sure you watch."

We meandered around the stream and ate some of the hush puppies of a few days back, quenched our thirst, and back to the trail we went. Most of the time we were silent and each kept our own thoughts. This type of silence felt natural, and there was no need to break it. There were many cutbacks and twists to the trail. At times, I lost sight of the small footpath, and at others, it appeared that nightfall had approached—so deep was the woods. Shoes forged ahead, and I watched as he became more winded and yet refused to stop. From somewhere in my small mind, I knew not to speak of his internal struggle; I could only watch in concern and admiration as this being harnessed a fortitude that I knew I would never possess.

After what seemed to be eternity, he stopped and unbridled his pack. Of course, I followed suit. He walked to one of the deadfall trees and sat. I waited until he motioned for me to take a break. Before I sat, I took one of the cans we had and went to get water. Returning, I took a small plastic bottle from my bag and filled it, handing it to him. Sitting on my bag, I waited for him to speak while listening to the area.

"Boy," he started, "we're about to go see a body. I call her the widow, met her some time ago, and we been friends since. She stays by herself, and when I come to the area, I make sure to go pay respects. I really don't know much about where she from and what caused her to be here or what keeps her here. Sometimes, it don't matter the road that a person had to take to come to any place. What matters is what they've become because of the journey."

I sat and listened. I knew this was a teaching, and though I wouldn't understand the lesson until years later, I knew enough to be attentive. It was in my awareness that this was important that I felt the foreboding that I had felt earlier. I breathed, yes, for breath, but also to calm my pattering heart.

"One time I was sick. And I'm talking the type of sick that kills a man out here if it ain't properly taken care of. I just happened to be in this area, and it had been a few days coming on. Being the noble hobo that I am, I figured it wasn't nothing I couldn't handle." He smiled at that. I smiled too. Then, continuing, he said, "I got to these woods, dragging and stumbling. Boy, I knew Shoes was going to be no more. I came to the place that we headed. The strange thing is that I had been to these parts times before, and never had I ever come across the widow's house. I'll be doggone in explaining it, but I never did, not until that fateful day or evening. I had stumbled out of a brush like a man that had crossed the desert when an old hound came toward me, and boy, I couldn't do nothing but let it get me! I didn't know I was on my knees till it sniffed at me and licked my face. The next thing I knew, I was looking up at a ceiling, lying by a fireplace. Shit, boy, I thought I was dead! Didn't feel quite like heaven, but looking at the fire, I figured I was close to hell!"

He and I laughed at that assessment of the situation.

"Anyhow, I lay real still, like I taught you. I was moving nothing but my eyes. From the far corner of the one room, I heard, 'If you done playing possum, maybe you might want something to eat!' Damn, boy, that scared the bejesus out of me, to the point I jumped damn near to my feet! Well, I didn't jump to my feet but was on my knees, backing up from the sound. While trying to get my feeble ass together, I heard the most beautiful cackling that could only be made by a woman. By God, I was in a woman's presence and scared shitless! Finally, scrambling to find where in tarnation she was and to get what manhood dignity I could get back, I scrambled so far back

I backed up into the damn fireplace. What the hell, boy, it was a mess! Capital letter M-E-S-S! Having singed my ass, I came to some sense and plopped down on the floor. I looked across the room, and there sat the woman in a chair, laughing, with tears rolling down her cheeks, attempting to wipe them with her sleeve. But she was holding a shotgun. I can tell you this, boy: things had gone from bad to a definite worse."

I was trying with all my might not to start laughing, but Shoes, seeing my futile attempt, beat me to the punch and started at a giggle—yes, grown men do giggle! He and I then ripped into gales of laughter. He was remembering the first meeting with the widow, and I was picturing the pair!

Shoes continued, "I sat there, and she told me to get my ass out of the fire. Between you and me, as I watched her cradle that shotgun, I knew I had a better chance in the fire as opposed to that gun. She asked how I was feeling, and I answered that I was feeling better than I did. As I was saying that, I started to stand, and the room went to spinning. And that was when she said, 'Fool, just sit there and get your bearings.' She asked if I thought I could eat a tad, and I said, 'Yes, ma'am.' At that, she chuckled and asked if I thought she was an old lady for me to call her ma'am. Well, shit, boy, I was old, and it appeared to me she was just as old, but on the other hand, she had a shotgun in her lap. I figured it might be best to come up with something that wouldn't get her finger to itching."

That was it for me; I screamed, and Shoes followed suit with rasping laughter.

After we settled down a bit, he said, "I told her, 'Ma'am, age ain't got nothing to do with calling a beautiful woman ma'am. *Ma'am* is the most polite and honoring thing that a man can say to a woman of your stature.' I thought that was pretty good, don't you, boy?"

Yes, I did think that was a great line, even if the shotgun wasn't the motivation!

"However, that woman couldn't be beat, boy. She, just as smooth as butter, said, 'And what type of stature would that be, Mr. Man?' as she and the shotgun leaned forward. Boy, I was in a pickle! She had me dead to rights. There was no way out of that box she done closed me in. I was defeated and buried, at that time, being the classy gal that she is, she let me off the hook by saying, 'Mister, you don't know when to shut up. I'm going to fetch you something to eat.' She and the shotgun got up out of the chair, and I sat there like a spanked child. I looked around the room and finally noticed the old hound that had licked my face before I passed out. That old hound had witness every word of that talk and gave me the look as if he had understood every word, and also, he looked at me as though I was a damn fool for thinking that I could pull the wool over the eyes of his woman. I could do nothing but agree!

"There was a rustling on the other side of this room, over where an old wood-burning stove sat. The woman spoke with her back to me as she went about getting me something to eat. 'You got to watch out for some buckshot in this rabbit. I made stew today, and stew is best for you now. I think you got some walking numona [pneumonia]. Probably be a couple of days till you start feeling any strength. If you want, you can stay on till you get better.' I had traveled far and wide up until that time, but I had not come across a single woman in a set place that was holding her own, without drifting in her own head.

"Over the days of my recovery, we talked, or at least she had me talk of where I'd been and the things I had seen. She didn't talk much about her past or where she had come from. She did let me know her man had died, that she was happy with him. You know, boy, I often wonder if that shotgun had something do with him being laid to rest, but I kept that, to myself."

I asked, "Mr. Shoes, how long you been knowing the widow?"

"Been about ten years, boy, that I've traveled to see her. Sometimes, I see her twice a year. I tried to get her to take small trips with me, but she says that she has seen as much of the world as she wanted. She's happy to have the peace of home." With that, he drifted off into his own mind and left me wondering about what would become of her. Did she have family? How could she get help if any was needed?

Shoes looked at me with distant eyes and spoke softly. "There are many things that man will never understand, and this is just one of them. That widow will die out here. The thing is this, boy: I don't understand what would make or have such a beautiful creature stay alone and isolated from this big world. Oftentimes I wonder if someone had hurt her real bad to cause this type of thing. When my mind goes along those lines, I get real mad."

"Is she your woman?" I asked.

"Boy, just like you or me, she's her own person. I am a man, and she is a woman." With that, he went silent, like that explanation explained everything! Later in life, I would find that those spoken words, indeed, were the truest of all explanations on relationships between men and women!

"Come on, we got to get to moving. Need to be there before nightfall. Around dusk, she changes out that buckshot for some four aught, says it makes bigger holes."

I didn't need any further explanation; I knew before the sun was down we'd be at our destination, or at least Michael would be sleeping in the safety and comfort of the forest.

We readjusted our packs, took a leak, and continued our march toward the widow. It was just as Shoes said: I did lose my sense of direction and at times wondered if he knew. I did take comfort and assurance that he was feeling better; hid movements were decisive, and he kept the look of determination on his face. After another hour at this pace, he held his hand up for a halt. He then walked to a dead-fall tree and began removing his sidesaddle. I stood, breathing deeply, and waited for him to give me the go-ahead to break. When he did, I found a position opposite of him so that we could see each other's back for safety. Seeing that I was in listening mode, Shoes took a sip of water from the plastic bottle.

"We be coming to the widow's property pretty soon. When I give you the signal, you hold back in the brush until I talk with her. Now, you make sure that you keep me in sight. There are two things that will be happening at the same time. One, it'll give me time to see what's what up close, and the second, it gives you time to cut and run or go karate on someone's ass if need. Boy, even though you might be familiar with a place, never put your guard down until you know it's all clear. Now, listen up, don't be taking just anybody's word for it. Remember, there's a lot of dead niggers that depended on some else's word!"

Several things came to me. I knew that Shoes trusted me and that I had come to know that he had my back, no matter what the odds. Also, he had given me permission to run if the odds were out of our favor. Later, I would learn that on the road, it was not in bad form to leave your partner, especially if both were certain to die. At least if one got away, then retribution could be had in honor of the fallen. However, the circumstance had to be extreme before you abandoned your comrade. It was just the law of the land. I knew that no matter the opposition, I would fight to my last in defense of my mentor; someone else would have to tell the tale or seek retribution.

I let him know that I understood, then began to look around at the trees and shrubbery.

Shoes sat awhile and rummaged around in his bag and then replaced the bottle in it. The evening was approaching, and we still had good daylight, so I didn't fear the widow's shotgun. As I watched Shoes from the corner of my eye, he seemed like a schoolboy going off to see his girl. It was a kind of fidgetiness that I remembered when I had sweethearts or lustful thoughts. I think, it was real compassion, because when we started again on the trail, I could see how he walked and the certainty in his step. I smiled to myself and told myself that I wouldn't be a third wheel or underfoot of these two. Actually, I kind of envied him. He was able to take a sabbatical from the road while yet still on it.

On occasion, I'd catch a whiff of wood burning and other aromas mixed with it. Though Shoes said nothing, I knew we were getting close. Shoes held up his arm like you see them do in war movies, causing a platoon halt. He turned to me with a nod, then began stepping into the thinning brush. While Shoes began his exposure to the property, I started to move quietly among the concealment that I could keep a visual. I observed a somewhat-overgrown thatch of land, a rough-hewn log, a block cabin, a well, few chickens pecking about, and a large brown dog napping on the front stoop. As Shoes neared, the dog became alert, not barking, but proceeding to meet

Shoes, who continued to walk at a slow, steady approach and began speaking with the animal.

"Hey, old boy, how you been?"

When the dog heard its name, it began to wag its tail. Sniffing Shoes's hands, and with small licks, it continued in a semicircle about him, with accompanying sniffs to his pant legs and crotch. After the greeting to the hound, he continued to walk toward the well. At that distance, I could see it clearly, and it even had a lowering bucket that sat upon its wall. Under the small well's roofing, which was supported by sturdy six- or eight-inch timbers, there were three items hanging by long nails. A dipper with a long ladling handle, a cowbell, and a wooden dowel, maybe an inch to an inch and a half in diameter and at least a foot long. Shoes lifted the dowel and began to tap out our Morse code. He waited for an interval and repeated it and then stood stock-still, with the dog beside him. While he was tapping, I eased even farther around, attempting to determine if any foul was lurking about. At the present moment, it appeared that I was the only lurker. I more so heard before I saw the heavy wooden door begin to pull open. The dog finally barked, letting whoever was behind the door know that he was on the job. Shoes hesitantly stepped forward, and the dog left him, headed toward the opening door. A woman stepped onto the stoop, in an apron and a dress that reminded you of the Old West days. I could see that her hair was a mixture of gray and black pulled into a tight bun. To this day, I cannot tell you the origin of her descent, but she was stately and, in a true form of womanhood, elegantly beautiful. Her strength and poise dictated nothing but respect. The demand of this respect was not by her; it was just something you were compelled to do.

The dog leisurely took up its position beside his mistress and casually lay at her feet. Shoes took his hat from his head and began to speak with her in tones that I couldn't hear. She and him spoke for some moments, and though I could not decipher what was being said, I could the quality of her voice. It appeared that they spoke in greetings and then past to the happenings in each of their lives since last they spoke, and then regarding the reason for this visit. I sat on a stump nearby and watched the courting of these two, and I also watched the chickens pecking and the birds leaping quietly among the branches. I felt the cooling of the late summer and the coming fall temperature. I watched, and after more moments had passed, Shoes called to me in a normal tone, "Boy, come meet the widow."

As I started out from my concealment, she turned her head in my direction and smiled. Even at that distance, I could feel her warmth. However, it didn't stop me from looking for the shotgun I had been told about. I didn't see it, so I continued toward Shoes and stopped about half a foot behind him and removed my hat.

"Widow, this here is the boy. He saved my bacon back yonder, and so I figured that this tenderfoot needed some teaching on road life. Boy, this is the widow, and a good friend of mine."

Looking in the direction of her face but not into her eyes, I said, "Pleased to meet you, ma'am."

She smiled and said, "Pleasure's mine, boy."

Again, I was amazed at this class of people who honored one another. With that small exchange between us, the dog stood and yawned and came off the porch to approach me. This did not alarm me, because I knew he was making his acquaintance with me. He sniffed my leg, and then my hand. At the moment of me touching him, a memory came just like greased lightning! When I was a child, my family had a hound just like him; his name was Brutus. Brutus was the first dog of my memory, with long drooping ears, long folded skin on his face, and drooling tongue! It was as though this hound suddenly recognized me as a long-lost friend and began wagging his tail. It was probably my imagination, but I had an immediate affection for the beast.

As I patted and talked to him, the widowed said, "You boys have been skunked. Ya'll make your way to the tack house and I'll boil some water, and you can wash before feeding time."

Shoes spoke up. "Got some stuff to kill what's left of the smell. Would you have a touch of lye?"

"I keep some for soapmaking. Go and show the boy the tack and I'll fetch it," she said.

"Come on, boy, we got to get busy," he said as he turned to go around the house.

Moving from where we stood, the chickens scattered but continued scratching. One chicken stayed with the dog, and where the dog went, the chicken stayed close to him. At that time, I didn't really think of that; it just was another passing curiosity, but a story would be told of their unique relationship!

Leaving the front, we passed the well, and as we turned the corner, a lone-standing building with a small window and wooden door sat behind the main house; farther away was an outhouse. Upon reaching the tack, Shoes opened the door to a room that I estimated to be twenty feet by twenty feet square. A small table, two chairs at the table, one hurricane lamp, a dangling light, and a bed, which was made. The miscellaneous other items were a piss pot and washbasin and some cups, plates, and whatnots. The room was snug and clean. We put our packs on the floor, and Shoes told me to follow him. Trailing behind, we headed toward the house. In the back of it, two large old metal tubs hung from nails on the back outside wall. Shoes directed me to carry them toward the middle of the yard, telling me that he would go to the widow and start preparing the fumigating ingredients. Before leaving me to the chore, he also told me to start filling one tub with water and to use the bucket at the well to go to the stream. I asked, "Why to the stream when the well is there?" He explained that the well water was for drinking and food preparation. Of course, in my mind I was thinking that he and I had been drinking stream water and washing in it for some time, but I did what I was told to do.

After about my seventh or eighth trip to the stream, Shoes came out of the house with a pot of a strange-smelling concoction and set it beside the empty tub. He said, "This will clean all our belonging. Now, go knock on the door and tell the widow you come to get the other hot pots."

I knocked and was permitted entry; she directed me to two large pots on the woodstove and told me that the one in the firepit was to go too. Carrying the first out, I was instructed to pour it slowly into the tub as he poured the contents from his. He stirred the brew with a wooden spoon to thoroughly mix it. I went back for the second and continued the process. The pot or kettle in the firepit was larger, and

I really had to heft it, but I was able to do it with only mild scalding, which motivated me to hold it steady. All the while Shoes stirred all the contents thoroughly. When he pronounced it ready, it was time to gather all our meager garments for cleaning. The lady had come on to the stoop and told Shoes that he should be able to find some clothes underneath the bed for us to wear while we did our laundry. We went back to the tack and found two pairs of long johns, the old one-piece sets. They even had the behind trapdoors on them. They were made for a large man, and once I had mine on, I had to roll the sleeves and the legs, making me look like a circus clown, and Shoes looked just as pitiful in his. He must have known what I was thinking, because he said, "Boy, I know you just met the woman, but don't be all embarrassed because you be wearing your drawers in front of her. Hell, I know it don't look dignified or proper, but we got to do what we got to do."

I knew that, and no, it didn't make me feel any better. So I did what I could and said, "You first." He shook his head and laughed and began gathering his clothes while I did the same and headed to the laundry mat by the well. When we rounded the corner, the widow was sitting in a chair on the small stoop. Embarrassment at the fact that I was in underwear, let alone the fact that I was wearing someone else's, caused me to slow down at the sight of her. She whooped out and said, "I do declare that boy done turned two shades of red!" She let out a musical tone of laughter, and in return, Shoes turned to look at me, trying to hide behind my bundle of smelling, skunked clothing. He did a double take and burst into laughter until tears fell. I wasn't laughing; there wasn't anything funny to me, and I was thoroughly done! However, the thing that kicked a man when he was down was when that old hound did a small howling sound, and the damn chicken came clucking at me and began pecking at my rolled-up long john leg. That started me into a laughing fit. Lord have mercy, sometimes fact is stranger than fiction! You just can't make stuff like this up!

Finally coming to our senses, we began the deskunking. Shoes explained that when tomatoes or tomato juice, gasoline/kerosene, lye, and bleach or alcohol are mixed, it will make everything fresh as a daisy. We stirred the clothes in the tub with a long stick and added hot water and let them sit after fishing them out. We wrung and carried them to the stream to rinse and did the process again. After we came back from the stream the second time, we placed the items into the second tub of fresh water. After that, Shoes explained that he and I would carry the washtub concoction closer to the stoop and wash down the door and windowsills and pour the mixture along the base of the front of the house and continue around the house until we had run out. The reason was that the mixture would help prevent critters from roosting, and snakes would stay away. If you could imagine the smell of it, you could believe that what he said had to be true, that it was a pesticide.

By the time we were though with the extermination detail, we returned to the rinsing tub, stirring and agitating the contents and wringing them, then set them on the ground. We did the same exterminating procedure with the water in that tub. Completing the task, we replaced the tubs in their place. Returning to the clean clothing, we gathered them and headed to the stream for the final rinse. A makeshift clothes line which hung between two trees concluded our laundry detail for the evening. Once done with that, Shoes walked me to the outhouse and explained that our detail for tomorrow would be to clean and burn. I was not looking forward to that! He explained the kerosene lamp would be the only light if I had to use the outhouse at night and that I needed to keep my eyes peeled for snakes at that time. There was electricity on the property, but the widow used it at a minimum and we should do so as well. The cowbell started to ring, and Shoes said it was dinnertime and it wouldn't be proper to keep a lady waiting.

I said, "Shoes, what can't be proper is sitting with a lady in someone else's underwear at her table."

"Well, you be dead right about that, boy, but it don't look like we got a choice," said he with a chuckle. "Don't worry, I'll lead this parade without you asking," he added with a smile.

The house was built like a rectangle containing a large kitchen and sitting area in one room. A wall had been built from rough-cut timber to what I presumed to be a sleeping space. At the doorway of the entry was a heavy drape that blocked the view. In the dining space was a large long table that accommodated four chairs. I stood with Shoes at the front and waited for the welcome in by the woman. She told use to rinse our hands in a pail of water on a stand by the stove and to seat ourselves. Shoes sat at the head of the table, and I sat to his left. The widow brought over a cast iron skillet with a top on it and returned to the stove and started to remove some homemade biscuits from the oven. All the while I felt as though I was an intruder in romantic moments that would have to be postponed. The fragrant odors and the grumbling of my stomach overruled any of these trepidations. The widow brought a glass pitcher of a pale substance, and when her trips to and fro were complete, the table was fully stocked.

When she approached the table after her transport of her labors, Shoes stood. I followed suit, and he pulled out her chair and she thanked him and sat. I waited for both of my hostess and host to be seated before I sat. My mind immediately remembered the teaching of my mom and dad repeatedly demanding that we learn the fundamentals of etiquette. After she requested that Shoes bless the food, the feast fit for a king began. I can't recall all that we ate, but I do remember how I felt sitting at that table. The warmth and care, the tolerant compassion of these two strangers, it made feel at home and simultaneously miss my home. Our conversation was light and continuous, and occasionally they would ask if one had seen this or that about or from a mutual acquaintance. It was one of the finest meals that I had had in quite a while. To this day, I compare an affair, when I am invited to attend one, to that night. Most of the time, that night was one beyond compare.

Once we finished the meal, the widow turned to me and said, "Son, that's apple cider. I know you and this old fool ain't been getting your nourishment. So I spiked that homemade brew with some of that moonshine to help get your inners in line. Y'all be here for a few days, and I'm going to see that some meat and strength get on your bones and vitals inside you. You and him going to get some dosings before you leave, starting in the morning, because I ain't having no dead bodies on my property!"

"You in for it now, boy!" said Shoes as the widow told him to stop his nonsense and eat.

I smiled as she smiled at me and continued to eat her portions.

I kept my eyes on my food, spoke when spoken to, and listened to them talk. It was just another family sitting for an evening meal. When we had eaten our fill, I asked if I could help in the cleanup and how I should start. Shoes told me to go get a bucket of water from the well; the widow had a pot of warming water on the stove already. We could use my bucket for rinsing. I was quite happy to be able to leave them alone for a spell and quickly excused myself.

Outside it had cooled, but it was not uncomfortably cold. The moon wasn't full and cast enough light for me to see the well-worn path toward the well. While I lowered the bucket, the old dog came to me, wagging his tail, and that chicken was with him. I kept my eye on the chicken, but it was just doing what chickens do, clucking around and scratching, pecking at the ground. I got the bucket and hefted it from the well's edge and started back to the house, followed by the dog and the chicken. Politely and lightly knocking on the door to announce my presence, I opened the door and both chicken and dog went in while I reached for the bucket, which I had set down to knock. I figured I had violated some type of law by allowing the dog to enter without permission, and there was no way to explain the chicken! Carrying the water to a large tub designated as a dishpan, I spoke to apologize for letting the dog in and really poured the excuses in apologies for the chicken.

"Son, that's just fine. Both of them normally sleep in here with me," replied the widow.

"Widow, you might want to tell the boy the story. If not, he's going to interrogate me to no end!" Shoes said. "Boy, come over here and sit so she can tell you, so you won't be bugging me!"

Wanting to hear this tale, I came to the table and sat across from the widow as Shoes added some more of the moonshine to his cider. The widow started, "A while back, a fox had come up on the place and had killed a couple of chickens. Took a while before old dog there was able to get him, but in the end he did. Now, while that critter was terrorizing me chickens, I took to bringing them in for the night before I could catch that rascal. During one of the nights before old dog could get him, one of my laying hens had gone missing, so I kept the eggs warm by the fireplace, in that box that the chicken is sitting in right now."

I sent my eyes roving to the overshadowed corner she had pointed to, and sure enough, that bird was sitting in it, next to the dog.

She continued, "One night, one egg hatched, and lo and behold, the first thing it caught sight of was the old dog, and that became its mama. Since then, I don't rightly know what it thinks it is, because what the dog does, it does. They're inseparable, and it's been that way since!"

I must have looked stupefied, because Shoes told me to close my mouth and the widow laughed her musical tone.

Later, the cleanup went smoothly, and I quickly removed myself under the guise of being tired, and my two elders didn't protest as I headed back to the tack house. With my belly full, and slightly tipsy from the cider and moonshine, I had no problem with the Sandman finding me. What was amazing was that I never once thought of that shotgun!

True to her word, after I had awakened and dressed again in the oversize long johns, I approached the house, hoping that I wasn't interrupting anything, because Shoes hadn't come back to the tack house. I loudly stepped onto the stoop and knocked on the door, hearing Shoes tell me to come in. When I opened the door, both canine and fowl exited. I watched them go into the front and closed the door behind them and turned to both Shoes and the widow at the table. After I greeted each, the widow said, "Son, you're right on time for your first dosing."

I looked, and on the table was a glass bottle with some thick liquid in it, and a large wooden spoon. I looked at Shoes, and he said, "I already had mine." I didn't believe him, but I wasn't in a position to argue, especially when the woman stood and motioned me to a standing spot and started unscrewing the cap, with wooden spoon in hand. She poured the most resistive liquid into the spoon and motioned that I open my mouth as she put that tree limb into my mouth and uplifted the handle, ensuring that I received all its content. With my mouth closed and my throat refusing to cooperate, the widow looked at me, waiting for the expected swallowing of the dosing. By Herculean powers, I forced my throat to swallow and went to gasp for air but was met with another spoonful. Shoes, who had been observing this, went from smiling to outright laughing as I was in the throes of trying not to vomit, while the widow pierced me with her dark eyes.

My life was over! There was no way anyone could live like this for any amount of time!

Finally able to swallow the last of the initial dosing, I began to feel the slow warming and then the fire of one of the main ingredients, moonshine, come shining through! I heard the widow ask, "Now, baby, do you want some breakfast?" I only had eyes for Shoes, who had gone from laughing so hard to a hacking cough. I was planning to get even with him. However, she brought him to reins when she told him that there was still enough for him if he didn't stop coughing. That comment got his attention!

We sat to eggs and salted pork and leftover biscuits with coffee. It was beautiful outside, and they both looked beautiful to me.

I must mention that we wore those long johns almost the entire period that we stayed there. The widow said it made no sense to stink up our clean clothing till it was time to leave. However, after close to four or five days working the way that we were, she recanted and demanded that we go bathe in the stream. While in the cool water, Shoes said, "Boy, those women, you'll never figure out. Just enjoy them while you can."

I believe we stayed a week, maybe ten days. I can tell you that homesteading is not for the faint of heart. My main duty was chopping wood for winter and gathering kindling piles to ensure that the queen of this dynasty would want for nothing in warmth. I found out what he meant by cleaning the outhouse, which the widow called a privy. By far, that was an experience, that doing it once was enough for me to always praise man for inside facilities. We had to tip it over and draw out the catch barrel, which was a fifty-five-gallon drum cut in half, and drag it farther from the house and, with kerosene, ignite and burn the fecal discharge. *Lord,* I mused, *what have I gotten myself into?* Once the burning was done, we dragged it downstream to an area and dumped, spread, and semiburied the contents and then started rinsing the half barrel and burning it again, then replacing it in the hole at the privy. Afterward, we cleaned the outside with soapy lye water, then the cleaning of the inside, and then, last the under half! I ate no lunch that day!

Each day we tasked till late afternoon. We ate good, and we slept good—at least I did, because Shoes never slept in the tack house. Each morning, just like clockwork, we had our dosings under the watchful eye of the widow. She even commented at one time that she couldn't trust us to do it ourselves. Believe me, she definitely spoke the truth on that note, because those dosings were honest-to-God dreadful moments that I never got used to! Being that I was assigned my task, I went about the best that I could. The dog and chicken were my companions. When the dog would lick my face or hand, the chicken would peck at my leg, hand, or any body part that it could reach. It was so bad that if I sat to rest and the old dog came to sit with me, that damn chicken would sit on the other side, occasionally pecking me. I got used to their companionship eventually and spoke often to each.

An evening came, after much of the winterizing and repair was done, when at dinner Shoes told me and the widow we'd be leaving in the morning. I knew that they had privately talked, so his making the announcement was for my sake and he hadn't said anything sooner because he knew how it would affect me. I didn't know that it would have the effect that it did, but he knew because of his time being on the road. Though I thought I was his protector, in truth, he was mine, and it was his job to birth me into the wisdom of road life.

"I've mended your clothes and have added a few things that will be easier to carry. I thank you both for all that you have done here," said the woman.

"Maybe it's best for you to turn in, boy," Shoes suggested. "We got to really travel at a good rate to get to where we be going."

Through the fog I heard this. I mumbled my "Good nights" and rose from the table. As I got to the edge of the table and the widow reached out, very gently, and took my hand, this time I looked into her dark eyes. And she spoke. "Boy, it was good meeting you, and I truly hope you find what you're looking for. Thank you for taking care of the ole goat. He's taken a strong liking to you. That means you're something special, because I know him. Get some rest and I'll see in the morning." With that, she stood and embraced me, kissing my cheek. She felt like my mother and gave me some of her strength, as mothers do.

Going to the tack room was a long, slow walk. I can't recall anything specific; it was only after sitting on the bed in the dark, while reaching to light that old light, that I remembered how she looked through her eyes. The same look was in Mary One-Eye, and it was the same look in the eyes of our tribe the day that Shoes and I left. It was the same—many variants, but the same look in each. I couldn't explain it then, but I can today.

I awoke to the familiar sounds of Shoes moving about. As I opened my eyes, the sun's rays streamed into the single pane, and the day was a gorgeous day for travel, though my heart was heavy with the weight of the pending departure. I watched as Shoes finished packing his bag and secured it, and then he went to the table, which had two cups of hot black coffee that still steamed, and sat. On the table was a plate covered by a checkered linen cloth. "That's breakfast for you." I swung my feet to the floor and padded to the washbasin in the corner to rinse my face and brush my teeth. After, I sat opposite my mentor and first sipped the coffee before removing the napkin to start to eat.

Shoes was silent, and I could see that there was something about his demeanor that had changed, then he began to speak. "I told you before there are a lot of goodbyes on the highway, and this is one of many more to come for you. So I'm going to tell you the proper way to always leave or have others leave you," he said. "Once the goodbyes are said and you go to moving on, never look back. It's said that if you do, you leave an essential part of you back there, and in times of real need, that part that has been left behind may become your undoing." He paused a bit. "I tell you, certainly the widow has taken a good shine to you, boy, just like me. She, in all her womanly ways, is afraid of what's before you and hope that you live to find what you searching for." I sighed. "So when you go to say goodbye, make sure you say it manly. This will give her comfort that it ain't no boy in front of her but a man. You understand what I'm talking about?"

I said, "Yes, sir," and continued to eat as he stood and looked out of the window, waiting for me to finish and get ready.

There were many things that ran through my mind. One was backing out when I first left home to marry, and how my mother carefully handled my new manhood decisions. I could feel the tears welling and fought with all that was in me not to let them fall. Shoes, still looking out of the window, said as an afterthought, "Ain't no shame in a man's tears. Anyone ever tell you different, they be lying. Tears clean you, boy. They clean from all the mud that the world throws at you." There were times that he was really mystical to me, and this was one of those times; but I still refused to cry, even though I was granted the liberty to do so.

We stood in front of the stoop as she and he made small talk. He told her that the plan was to get to Four Corners in two days' walk, maybe sooner if we could hitch a ride. What I remember most is how they continued to look at each other, thinking to myself just how much they loved each other and yet restrained to allow each to be their own person and master of their own fate, making their choices of how to live.

The widow spoke to me while I stood before her, and at this time, I did notice the shotgun leaning on the chair beside her. I answered mechanically and politely. Then, Shoes announced it was time to hightail if we were to make headway. With that, we turned away from yet another home and another tribe to meet the road. Never looking back, we silently walked the pathways, which appeared to be used more frequently.

After a while, Shoes extended his hand and placed a holding grasp on my arm. "Michael, you did good. Now, hold up just a moment." I looked questioningly at him as he held me in place, and then I heard the booming single sound from the blast of the shotgun. He said, "Come on, boy. It would have been bad if that blast hadn't sounded, and worse if it blasted twice. Pick 'em, boy. We got to clear the area."

CHAPTER 18

Four Corners of Fate

We had a good time on the well-worn pathway, and Shoes led us away from the streambed and mentioned we were to come to a dirt road and maybe be able to hitch a ride. He told me, when hitching, always to continue walking in the direction of traffic, just in case you don't get picked up, you'll still be making time. He also explained the shotgun blast as being a signal that friendlies were leaving the haven and were to be granted safe passage. I had been a fool to think that the widow lived this far from civilization without the protection from a tribe. I felt better, but still foolish!

After we had spent a few hours walking on a steady pace, a farmer on a tractor pulling a long bed cart told us to hop aboard and that he could take us as far as his turnoff. We climbed aboard and rode in silence. I watched the land, which was beautiful, roll past as we bumped and jostled in the wagon-like cart. Turning to ask Shoes some questions that were on my mind, I saw that he had fallen asleep, so I remained quiet. About five miles of slow tractor riding, the farmer hollered back that his turnoff was up ahead. He slowed enough for us to hop down, and we said our thanks. He then continued into his turn down a dusty hollow.

We walked the road, and Shoes shared a great many things. Most of the information was new, and some had been rehashed from previous lessons. After a couple of hours, he estimated we had covered twenty to twenty-five miles and that we should rest a spell. Going into the brush from the roadway, he found a small sunlight clearing and situated his bag into a makeshift pillow and began unlacing his shoes. I followed his unspoken lead and did the same. Pulling my socks off to air my feet, I began inspecting my bag. Shoes began speaking.

"Everybody that travels the road need to have a soul song of their very own. The reason is that, dependent on where you are going, most of the time you're by yourself. To walk with that much quiet and stay in it, you could let your mind run away from you and become as crazy as a shithouse rat! Boy, we ain't got a lot of sense to begin with, being out here like this in the first place, but to bug out on the road is bad for you and anyone that comes in contact with you. It gives a bad name to those of us that are already thought of as good-for-nothing tramps. Since the dawn of time, man has always created music of some sort. You know, music is how we come close to God, and music keeps us real close to being as balanced as we possibly can be. Now, many of us ain't got no instrument to play. Hell, most couldn't play one if we did, because we never learned. Everyone, boy—and I mean *everyone*—has a soul, and that soul speaks in words, but music moves it. So you got to get your 'soul song,' and it will keep you company when you be by your lonesome."

The things that he was saying made sense to me. I remembered, prior to meeting the tribe, there were times that I began to hum or sing songs that I had made up. I wondered whether that was some type or kind of a soul song. Naturally, I thought of the spirituals that in church we used to sing. I asked, "Do you mean like the wretch song we sang in the mission, or some old Negro spirituals?"

He answered, "Boy, if those be the type of songs to bring you comfort, faith, and strength, they'll be as good as any. However, after a time of being out here, a person got to get something that's only his. This way, whatever mojo it has, is his and his alone." He began by humming his tune, which he carried. It sounded like a spiritual, or maybe even it came from some part of it, but the way he tuned it out was heartfelt. There were variations of it, which he explained had to do with whatever task he was about doing. I was too self-conscious to try at that time, so we walked and he hummed, our feet keeping rhythm. I learned that the Indians had something called their death song, which would help usher them into the big hunting ground or encourage them in times of war to be fearless. Believe it or not, I believed it then, and to this day, I have created or evolved my own "soul song." I found that his explanation of this mysterious phenomenon proved to be true.

After a few more hours, Shoes said he was tuckered out and that before the sun got too low, we needed to shelter for the night. Up ahead he spied a copse of trees, and we headed for them. Once among them, I was told to gather some kindling that we could use to make a small fire. We made do with what was at hand, and it was in no time we were set for the night. That night, Shoes continued his extrapolation on what knowledge I needed for the future. His dialogue was both captivating and detailed, and it wasn't until the crest of the waning moon held high in the clear sky that he said we better stretch out for the rest of the night because we had a good ways to go and needed to hump on tomorrow. I lay awake for a while, listening to the night, until I heard his gentle snore. My last thought was of what would become of this adoptive father figure, as well as what would become of me. Though I was still new to this strange world, I also knew all things came to an end. With that last thinking, I passed into the gentle night.

In the morning, I awakened to a chill, and the morning was overcast. Shoes was still on his side, facing from me. Just for a moment, a dread grasped me with a thought that he might have died, but quickly, maybe too quickly, I dismissed the thought. Yet I lay still to check if I could see the rise and fall of his shoulders, to ensure he still lived. Assured that I wasn't alone, I sat up and rubbed my hand across the dew on the grass and vigorously rubbed the moisture on my face. Getting up and moving from the camp, I relieved myself against one of the trees. Then I padded back and saw that Shoes had awakened and was sitting up, going through his bag. Greetings of "Good mornings" were passed, and then each of us proceeded to do what had to be done personally before the day could be entered properly.

His plan was simple. First, we eat a cold breakfast, then inventory our stock between us and move out. That simple plan lasted for another thirty-mile track that day. We walked, hitched, and even caught a rail (train) heading to Four Corners. While on the train, we met and traded small supplies with other tribal members. As we waited to hop off at an upcoming slow bend, Shoes told me why the place that we were headed to was called Four Corners by our population. I thought that was the name of the town and found out that it was named something else. To this day, I don't know its name; however, it will forever be Four Corners to me. I become comfortable with the name, so Shoes and I just referred to it as the Corners.

It had started to mist, rain as Shoes told the tale of this place. Long ago, when hoboing was popular and quite a common thing, the population, like any other thriving civilization, needed rules and rulers. Rulers came in all sorts; some came by votes, others by force and fear, and still others by heroic acts. Hoboing is pretty much a territorial adventure; before long, there were wars between who had what and how far their territory was. So like in any other thriving society, the top hobos met and divided the nation into four parts. He said that Four Corners was the meeting place and that, actually began the territories. I was to be heading south, and he said he had to head west. In Four Corners, one could get updated information on what was happening and where, this was good to have foreknowledge of your destination. I do not know if that was true, but I reminded myself that as far as I could tell, he hadn't lied to me as of yet, and most things that he had told me, I had witnessed with my own eyes.

We settled for the duration, and the rocking of the train eased us into a comfortable state. Shoes produced a small airplane bottle of clear liquid, swigged about half, and handed it to me. About an hour later, the long, slow whistle began to blow. Shoes told me to gather our stuff because we had almost ten minutes before the bend and then we would exit. While we readied and stood by the cargo door, the misting rain had stopped; you could see that the ground cover was wet. The whistle sounded again.

Shoes looked at me and said, "Boy, promise me something. I want you to promise me that when you hear a train whistle blow, no matter where you are, I want you to know that I'm near. Most people ain't remembered, and I can't say I'm worth remembering, but just the thought that there is someone trying to remember me gives me a good feeling."

I didn't hesitate to affirm that I would do it. He smiled and once again repeated what he had told me about taking his shoes and bag. That if it made me feel any better, he'd be willing them to me. He said that this was the way of the highway and this was the best that we could do for each other. The uneasiness that had been with me on and off was definitely on now. We had discussed these things several times over the weeks, but it seemed as though there was a sense of urgency beneath his calm tone. Again, I kept these thoughts to myself as he said, "Curve's up 'head. Jump after me. It'll be rolling slowly."

At that time, there were several other men in the car with us, though each of us was amiable to one another, we stayed in conversation with our own. The thing about rolling out of a boxcar is that you do not roll out on a curve, in the inside of the turn; you always roll on the outside so that the wind doesn't catch you and throw you under the rails. You always look for curve jump-offs most of the time so as not to be seen by the engine driver or the guard dogs watching for hitchers. The main objective is to be ninja: unseen, unheard, leaving no mess. No matter what territory you travel, the prime directive is to respect "normal" society and their rules so that there is no backlash on our subculture. Punishment for violating this rule was severe.

Shoes said, "Here we go, boy." And with that, he leaped. We were moving at a slow speed, but since I had never jumped from a moving train, I momentarily held my position and watched Shoes as he leaped, ran, and dropped and rolled. It was a spectacular sight! As he stood, I leaped, attempting to imitate his grand performance. Leaping, I sensed my first foot touching the ground was a trip, my second step a stumble, the third the beginning of a fall, and arms outstretched, the body slam and half-roll, and then flat on my back. As I lay on gravel and grass, I could hear Shoes and those that had exited laughing so hard that all I could do was laugh while lying there! My one of many rail jumps. Subsequently, I, to my fortune, have improved my technique.

Walking toward me with one other man in tow, Shoes was wiping tears from his eyes as the other was still heartily laughing. Not being injured, nothing but my pride, I was standing and brushing the rail debris from my clothes. Shoes and the other stood before me, and Shoes made introductions. "Whiskey, this is the boy. Boy, Whiskey."

Whiskey extended his hand and laughingly said, "Boy, you sure know how to make an entrance, don't you?"

"Yes, sir, always been unforgettable," I said, smiling back as I shook his hand.

I picked my bag up, and the three of us started our walk in the same direction. Whiskey and Shoes spoke together, and I followed behind respectfully. Occasionally, either Shoes or Whiskey, out of courtesy, would fling me a bit of conversation. I wasn't bothered with being excluded, because I knew they were exchanging pertinent information and getting information that would be useful to self and others. But after some time of walking with us, Whiskey announced he'd be taking a turnoff but would probably meet up with us at the Corners. Before he left, he asked if it would be okay to give me some pointers on rail jumping.

"Don't mind if you do," replied Shoes. "I be needing a break."

Veering from the tracks into the woods, Whiskey found a spot that was clear and had a small rising ground to practice rolling.

In a general way, this was what happened. Whiskey took center stage as Shoes sat propped against a tree, but I had to stand ready to mimic anything that Whiskey threw my way. "One of the first things you got to do is practice rolling. Now, you ain't got to be on a train to practice rolling. Anytime and anywhere you find yourself, it's always a good idea to practice rolling. Whether a train, bus, car, horse, or even just walking, you got to practice! The surface tells you how to roll and land. You got to factor in things such as speed of motion or sun, rain, or cold."

Oh my god, he had made this a course on the science of rolling! He demonstrated and had me do it over and over. Running, walking, up the knoll, down the knoll. It went on and on. By the time we were finished, Shoes was sound asleep, with his head resting on his pack out. Whiskey said there wasn't a need to wake him but to let him know that they'd catch up at the Corners, as we actually called it.

While I watched him slide away, I realized I had seen moves like that in karate, kung fu, judo, and other martial arts schools for years, and yet this disjointed person from humanity had perfected an offensive and defensive maneuvering better than some of the best masters! Turning from Whiskey's exiting path, I started to heft my bag and awaken Shoes. Walking toward him to do so, I stopped. My mind began to replay some of the previous days' scenes before me, and what I saw over and over was that Shoes was taking more and more rest periods. As I continued to review the film footage, I also reviewed his facial features, his body movements, and the gait of his strides while we traveled. I was angry at myself for not being able to immediately recognize that, indeed, my beloved friend was struggling. It was in this twinkling of revelation that I decided that this would be our nesting site for this night. No matter how he protested when he would awaken, I would stand my ground.

Turning from him, I estimated about how much daylight was left and knew that if I got busy, all things could be in place. Gathering kindling, scouting material for a cover, and rifling and scourging for edibles, I knew a meager but sustainable meal could be had. By the time my mentor awoke, which he did with a start, I had all preparations made and was sitting beside him. I placed my hand on his arm as he jump-started himself to begin to attempt to make up time for the hours he slept away. Restraining him gently, but with a firm grasp, I asked, "Why didn't you tell me?"

He went to jerk away, but I held him fast.

"Why didn't you tell me, Shoes?"

He ceased his struggle against my ironclad grip and, at first, looked me dead in the eyes and then dropped his head toward the ground. I released him when he stopped his struggle and listened as he took in a deep, soothing breath, sighing. "Boy, I knew that you would do exactly what you're doing now!"

"And what is that?" I asked him in return.

"This! This is what I knew! That you would forget all your learning and start trying to redirect the traffic of what's natural!"

"Damnation, man, can't you just once—just fucking once!—just speak in plain ole English so I can understand what in the hell you are talking about and trying to hide?" I didn't shout but said it in the enough-with-the-esoteric-bullshit, get-straight-to-the-point tone.

He raised his head and looked into the trees. "I know that something ain't been right about me for some time now. However, being the great I am that I am, I nursed myself all these years, so I just kept nursing."

I remained silent because I knew enough not to interrupt; I could always ask questions later. As the forest began its transition toward evening, Shoes continued, "Over the last few years, I started to get winded more easily. Sometimes I couldn't think straight or remember what I was doing or was supposed to do. You know, small things."

I nodded in agreement, understanding him. Though my outer appearance was a mask of listening without interruption, my inside boiled with emotion! Yes, I had expected the clearing of the slate in being kept in the dark about him feeling bad over the past few days and keeping it from me. However, I was not prepared for the fatal information that he was now giving! The dilemma now existed on whether I would interrupt in shock and fear of being left alone or if I could remain contained and silent as he confessed the litany of his life.

I do not know whether it was because I found the courage not to think about myself or whether it was God that kept me silent and still. Whatever the cause, I was his sounding board as he spilled his life discourse. What I do know is that I absorbed his tale just like a sponge, at first resistant, then the longer in the pool of liquid, I yielded my dryness of ignorance to empathetic absorption. I wanted to hold on to what would become of me if I lost this beacon light. I really couldn't hear because my overruling emotions roared so loud! What I am relaying today is, in hindsight of what was said, I believe that would be the first of many times that my emotional constitution would hear and interpret information that, in its magnificence, has always stayed with me, only to reveal itself at the appointed time, this time. I could feel the process of symbiosis as he released and I absorbed. We balanced each other in those moments. This is the best that I can explain. In the end, he concluded this cascading discourse with, "Now, boy, you know that we become the sum total of all that we experience and choose which pieces we are to keep."

I sat across from him as the low fire burned, and watched the shadows dance in his eyes and over his face. Did I see him somewhat a little more withered and tired after the telling of his tale, or was my mind creating yet another catastrophe? The answer was both yes and no; however, I was too young to know. However, time, as the patient teacher of all, would have her lessons learned. This is true with us also who are not the most astute of students.

I passed him the bottle for our evening ritual. Shoes expectantly kept his eyes on my every move, knowing that I was digesting the largest of all the lessons that he taught me. Taking our shared bottle back as he handed it to me, I said, "Old man, thank you. As you have been telling me, all things come to an end. So where do we go from here? I mean, do you have folks you want me to contact? I mean, what do we do now?"

He said this in a very contented tone: "We still got time. We'll talk in the morning and along the way. But, son, it's simply that I die, you live. It ain't nothing but the natural."

It might have been my exhaustion, but that sat right in me and we ended the day.

The following morning had cooled, and Shoes was already up when I woke up. I was not able to determine how long, but it was long enough for coffee to be made and to have cold corn pones. Four Corners was still several days' destination, and we had come to a truce unspoken. It came about on its own accord, so I'll just summarize our days.

Noticeably so, Shoes had deflated. I surmise that no longer having to keep up the ruse of power, he had succumbed to mortality. I do not believe that at any time was he ever in denial, but he was truly concerned for me and what life was going to present me. Him not knowing whether or not I'd be able to stand, he did what any protective parent would do, defy death itself, though it would win in the end. He wanted more than anything else to ensure that I had a fighting chance; this was even so at the cost of his last living strength.

Over the days of our travel, I learned that a year ago, Doc had been able to arrange with one of his contacts who worked at one of the local clinics to have Shoes unofficially get blood work, x-rays, MRI, and a host of other medical workups, unbeknownst to the tribe. The rusts read by medical professionals were final in the spread of what was called pancreatic cancer, mortality rate 100 percent. Swearing Doc to secrecy, Shoes had set about working on tribal affairs, that it would be sustained. My coming on the scene was in the twilight of the strategies acted upon. This, by no means, was easy for me to accept, and Shoes plainly spoke the truth of the matter. In essence, he said that all was as it should be. If I believed in a God, then it was that God that brought us together, and for some very good, commonsense reasons. First off, I was new to the trail; I didn't have any knowledge. Of course, I could fight, but that wasn't enough to ensure a good survivability rate. He, a dead man walking, knew his knowledge would die with him and everything that he possessed, bag and shoes, would go to someone else. At least this way, he could have a say-so to whom they should go. Sure, he had regrets and remorse, and yes, he would, if he could, change some things in his life. Here I comment that he never said what those things might have been. I, in turn, didn't ask. Conversationally, he spoke like everything was clandestine, and as I listened to him, I realized his words took the sting of my loss, my anger, and my fear down a couple of notches.

Throughout the days, we took frequent breaks and laughed at some of my newer days in the tribe life, and he spoke of his early years. I did notice that he never pinpointed places or people, and I did question why he told things the way he did. He did tell me it was because there are some things that hold no statute of limitations in the law and to tell places and specific things could cause harm to a good many people. Wow, I never thought of that, and perhaps as you read these escapades, you may be wondering where and when. Just know there was a when and where that these recounts are from, which what I know, not just make-believe.

It appeared the closer we got to Four Corners, the more Shoes withered. But never did I hear a complaint of discomfort, nor did he make me feel self-conscious as I fussed over him. He seemed to be amused by my bumbling attempts to minister to him. I did not verbally share my deep sadness with him. I tried the best I could not to have the fear that chilled my bones in all my waking moments surface. However, I know that he knew, because he would direct my attention to the things that I had learned, about the dos and the don'ts of the road life. At the end of these affirmations, he'd say, "That's my boy!" I would warm at that praise each and every time, comforted that someway, somehow, no matter what, he would always be there.

We made it to Four Corners about four days after Shoes had told me his secreted mission. In those four days, he had transformed from the world's greatest hobo to just another dying old man. Though the dignity and presence of mind remained evident, his body consumed himself, and he relied more heavily at his protégé and student in arms. It was as though, after he had given away his secret, it was now okay to pass on.

On the last leg of our journeys, we had hitched a ride in the back of a pickup. It had lightly started to rain, but not heavy enough for us to be invited to ride in the cab. As we continued our transport, it began to rain more heavily. As I began to lean to bang on the cab to get the driver's attention, Shoes stayed my hand and said, "Boy, you never overstep your bounds on hospitality!" I sat back and fumed silently at the driver, consumed in absolute terror at what the wetness was going to do with his deteriorating condition. I felt helplessly useless. I gave him a small wool shawl that I kept in my saddle and watched as it absorbed, more so than repelled, the droplets. I died inside.

Four Corners was nothing but a shantytown. Once one of the towns in which the citizenship was hopeful that the railroad would pass through. Yet like many municipalities that hoped that the rail system would contribute to commerce, it was a failed dream and hope. The railroad found it cheaper to bypass rather than to share the wealth. As a result, the small municipality existed on the river nearby and barges. The small population only hung on to die.

Shoes and I arrived late in the afternoon, and he led me to a small shanty of a building that resembled much like a working toolshed, minus tools, that might have been used in better days for construction of building, homes, roads, and maintenance project upkeep. At this time, it appeared just to be another decaying structure, which most of the township consisted of. I made Shoes as comfortable as possible, stripping him off his wet clothing and replacing them with a drier set. Leaving him for a few moments, I scoured the town's dumpsters and passageways for cardboard and any other burnable material. Making it back to our nesting site, I started a small warming fire and created a pad of cardboard for him to rest and sleep on. I knew that the bare cement floor would seep necessary warmth from him, and cardboard would be both mattress and added blanket against the cold. Having some of the widow's potent concoction left, with a small swig or two of moonshine, I was able to warm it and the small makeshift meal. Taking care of him first, I knew that we were in a bad state, because he didn't fuss but complied. The liquor and the widow's elixir took the immediate chill from him, and he was able to eat the meager meal. He wanted to doze off between bites, and I don't know if I kept him awake to finish the meal because I thought he truly needed it or because I was scared to death he'd die. That was one the longest nights of my life!

That night, I dressed him in my extra set of clothing and kept the fire higher than normal in the closed space. I'd snuggle close to him and cuddle him as a child. I did not think it strange or weird, nor did I feel any indecency about two men hugging during the night for warmth; my only thought was of him and his comfort. There were moments of complete anguish as I toiled to jar my memory on what my mom and the elders of my community had administered at times such as these during my childhood. Fitfully he slept off on and off. Occasionally, he'd wake up and say, "Boy, I ain't going to give you any nooky, no matter how good you treat me." I know that he knew we were fast approaching the end of our road. However, he didn't think of himself—he thought of me—while trying to lighten a situation that was immovable and of immense weight! I would only smile at him and say, "Old man, if you had any nooky to give, I wouldn't use

Digger's pecker to touch it!" He'd laughed, very lightly, and slip into another fitful doze. I knew he had a rising temperature, because he was hot to touch but at times shivered uncontrollably. At those times, I'd rub him vigorously and cuddle him tightly.

Somewhere during the course of the night, I began to hum and scat (Ella Fitzgerald made that type of music famous) his soul tune while rocking him gently on the cardboard bed. This did seem to have the desired effects, for he would rest more easily and the temp began to fall, his fitful sleeping appearing to deepen. By the graying of the sky, the weak sunlight poked through the various holes in the walls, the unevenly hung front door, and the paneless window. This was the beginning of a new day. Outside temperatures dropped before pushing the degrees up. I built the fire higher than safety pre-caution would have allowed, but I knew this was critical, and besides, I would be right here. I reheated more of the widow's remaining elixir and set our coffee sock in a can of water. I made sure that it was just a little water so that it could be stronger. It would be just enough for him. After I ensured that he'd be all right, I would make my foraging rounds, perhaps running into a few of the local nomads to barter, trade, and/or commission promissory notes. However, first things first: I had to be sure I could leave him alone for an hour.

After an hour of my preparing things in our makeshift encamp-ment, Shoes finally opened his eyes and yawned deeply. Watching him, I could see that he seemed refreshed and somewhat better, but I did not take this as a sign that we were out of the woods yet con-tending with this spell. I spoke up as he reached for the coffee. "Hey, old man, before the coffee, here, take this," I said, handing him the widow's elixir. He frowned, set the coffee back down, and drank what was in the smaller can, making extreme faces and gagging signs. "Damn, boy, you trying to kill me?" he said as he hurriedly sipped the coffee to combat the taste. We went back and forth in banter as I assessed him and he attempted to demonstrate that he was all right, at least not at death's door yet.

He told me that we needed to get out in the Corners to start getting what we needed. I rebutted and told him that I would go on the initial recon until he got his good legs back under him; it might not be a good idea going into an unknown territory with a handicap. I was quite surprised when he agreed. We agreed that an hour should be adequate time to look about and that upon my return and report, we could make a better-informed decision of what to do next.

After making sure an immediate relapse wasn't going to occur, Shoes gave me one immediate instruction, which was to ensure that local general store was still operational. It also held the post office. If it was not still in operation, I was to make sure I found where the post office was. Afterward, I was to travel to the Baptist church and to advise the minister that he was in town and would like to schedule a time to see him. After these two important tasks, I was to locate the locals and ask for supplies and whatnot. Accomplishing the first two agenda items with relative ease, I knew that approaching the local nomads would be more challenging. Shoes said to first try it on my own for practice, and if that failed, to drop his name. He explained that as a hobo, we must not depend on the reputation of others to win the day; we must make our own reputation by our own actions. I understood what he was saying; however, my main objective was to procure anything and everything I could for his well-being. This was by any means necessary.

I was taught to first start by finding the public transportation centers. These included bus stations, cabs, trains, boats, jitney services, and airports. All these had disenfranchised individuals that parasite off the mainstream. Second, grocery stores, restaurants, hotels, and bars; these provided discarded staples, which were actually leftovers and waste of the gluttonous. The third were pharmacies, clinics, and hospitals, in which I could find discarded health supplies. During all this recon, I was to take notice of seedy operations, such as drug distribution, prostitution, or outright signs of gang activity and police presence. Four Corners, as mentioned, had been settled in the hopes that the railroad would come through and bring the dollars with it. Of course, that was a failed hope, and the shantytown had ceded to the just-get-by status.

It didn't take long locating the local outcasts, and I found them to be cooperative. I used Shoes's name in each meeting. I knew this to be in violation of what he had told me, but the sense of urgency overruled the dictate of following his instruction. Reflecting on it now, I can say that I would do it the same if I had to repeat it. I was able to gather information, food, medicine, and a small bottle of liquor and receive word back from the pastor that he would be able to see Shoes at the rectory tomorrow after 8:00 a.m., but before twelve noon.

When I came back to our roost, Shoes was still sleep, and so I went about the small space, placing all the collected booty in its place. I had been able to get a couple of discarded pots and a frying pan. Cleaning the ashes from the previous night's fire and building a better fireproofing because I had time, I readied our new temporary home. During my hunt, I had found a blanket and other material to add to the makeshift cardboard bedding and found a pan deep enough to be used as a toilet, just in case. Finally satisfied, I sat a minute to collect my thoughts. My thoughts were no longer on heading south; for now, they centered on the old man. While sitting, I noticed that he had removed his shoes and slept in his stocking feet. The picture of this appeared to be normal, and yet I knew something was off about the scene. Though I couldn't grasp exactly what it was that had caught my attention, I could feel that it was important. However, this wasn't the time to tarry over anything elusive; I had to focus on what clearly needed to be done. Lunch, liquids, and the meager meds of aspirin, antibiotics, and liquor were needed for the slumbering man.

By the time he had started to stir, I had lunch of a sandwich and soup for him. I insisted that he take the last of the widow's elixir and asked about how he felt. He truthfully spoke of his decline and the lack of strength and his malaise feeling. I told him that I found a bottle of rotgut and that it, mixed with a stout cup of coffee, may help. Among other things not mentioned, I had been able to get fresh grounds of coffee that had never been used. The rotgut and fresh coffee appeared to do the trick, because Shoes removed his socks and began the foot ritual and, as he did so, explained that we needed to head to the post office. I went about the cleanup satisfied and relieved that he seemed to rally.

After he hung his socks to air and placed another pair on, I heard him chuckle. "Damn widow done sewed another hole up."

I said, "She cares for you, old man."

"Yeah, she do," came the quiet response.

We left our lodging and headed to the general store in which the post office was in. I had been with Shoes when he went to the post office before in our other locale. At that time, I had waited outside, but this time he said, "Come on, boy." Going directly through toward the small wood structure, I noticed there hung a sign that simply said, "Postmaster," and a counter sat beneath it. We stood for a moment, and then an older White man came from behind a curtained area and asked if he could help us. Shoes said, "Name is Shoes. I sho' have a general delivery." I stood there and kept my mouth closed. I knew you needed identification, you needed a name, maybe even a last name. I figured you needed something a little more than just saying, "My name is Shoes!" Well, apparently, I was wrong. And not only was I wrong, but I was also largely wrong, even if you can't be largely wrong! From behind the curtained area, I could hear the postmaster say, "You Shoes? You and your boy come get this stuff." Rounding the counter and entering the curtained spaced, I was thrown back to a simpler time. The post office cubbies held mail in sectioned spaces, the place smelled of Pine-Sol, and the wood was rich and dark and polished. On the floor sat a couple of satchels of unopened mail, and in a corner, directed to by the old man, sat maybe five plain-wrapped brown packages, some taped, and others bound in twine. He said that they belonged to Shoes and had been there awhile. I carried the bulk of it, leaving two small packs for Shoes, and we thanked the old man, who bade us a good day. In my astonished state of mind of what had just occurred, I was reeling from the back-in-the-day experience. Shoes commandeered the lead and led the way back to our roost. Our packages contained all types of supplies—dried meats, coffee, medicines from stores and root doctor kinds, socks, and even a blanket like throw, which Shoes said would repel water and keep a body warm. And there were more stock than I can remember. We spent a good part of the day separating and repackaging. He set aside things to be distributed in the community and had me note those who had been most compliant when I had approached them as a stranger and had given freely.

The days were easy, and Shoes seemed to be on a rebound, and yet he didn't appear to regain his vibrancy. We kept his meeting with the local pastor, and Shoes gave him some of our provisions for others and handed him a small amount of paper bills. The shantytown vagrants were a variety of sorts, and Shoes told me that most of hobo ways will be lost on the new breed. We were kind and cordial, and yet I noticed that he did not invite any to our fire, and neither did we stay at theirs. I questioned him on that, and the simple explanation was that we could do badly by ourselves. That was simple, but a clear dictate to always follow.

About four days of our stay, as I walked with Shoes, we heard, "Boy! Hey, boy, been doing any rolling?" To our surprise and delight, on the opposite corner stood Whiskey, grinning from ear to ear. Crossing the street, we met him curbside and exchanged greetings, and he and Shoes began talking. Shoes and Whiskey talked and walked intently, with me in tow; to my surprise, the walk led to our temporary home, and we invited him to coffee, a bite to eat, which was my signal to get busy and let grown folk talk and for me to get the bottles of mash for him and Shoes. Shoes had said to always invite one to drink because it loosens the tongue and oils the memory. We ate a light meal, had coffee, and drank. During that time, Whiskey spoke of his divergent path and gave Shoes information on his inquiries. As I listened, I couldn't make out anything important, but there were passages of the conversation on which he had Whiskey speak on detail.

As the dusk was settling, Whiskey told us that he had to get to his diggings by night because he'd be leaving early and had to meet some others early. As he stood to go, I asked, "Whiskey, which way are you traveling?" He stopped and looked at Shoes, who nodded his permission for Whiskey to tell me. And he said, "West, my boy. We be trailing west." I said, innocently enough, "Good luck," and continued my cleanup detail. He and Shoes spoke a little more by the door, and then he was gone. Busily cleaning and straightening our own digging, I began to hear Shoes's soul song being hummed. By the time I was done Shoes was already sitting upon the floor with his legs outstretched, sipping from one of the bottles in our stash. I knew this to be an invite to sit. Each night since our arrival, other than the first night, he always spent part of the evening before retiring transmuting information, detailed information that he said "would never lose its value," no matter which end of the social scale I would find myself. It was important, and maybe one day I'd thank him or God for it. I really don't know if I believed him then and whether or not it was out of respect for him that I sat as an apt pupil at the teacher's feet. What I have come to know is that he spoke the solemn truth.

As he handed me the bottle to catch up to his state of mind, I watched him drink the spirits of its content. He then began untying his shoelaces to remove his shoes. It came into my mind that this untying of his shoes and removing them, which had become a nightly ritual since our coming to Four Squares, was against the road traveling handbook which he was verbally transmuting to me. Each seasoned traveler knew to keep your shoes on during the night because you may have to move quickly and your feet need to be bound and ready! This had been one of the first dictates that he had spoken to me. He followed this at all times, except during our mission stay, which required showering before bed. Still, I accounted this breach of protocol as nothing. I was to find, however, that it really said it all. He began this night's discourse of the importance of respect and to remain kind. He went on to how to select a tribe and where to stay or not stay. He spoke about the hobo signs to look for, which could tell me what lay ahead. Finally, he spoke of walking alone if need be. He said if I wasn't good company to myself, I was worthless to anyone else. He said he believed that I would do just fine and that people along the way would benefit because of me. That comment made me feel uneasy, simply because I felt useless to myself. Winding down, he said, "Boy, you got to remember and do what I say, even if I ain't with you—I be talking from experience." I handed him the bottle, and he tilted it and drank deeply and said it was time for lights-out and gave the remnants of the drink back to me, saying "Good night."

It is said that hindsight is twenty-twenty, meaning that if one reflects on past experience, one would find that everything was being told to you in the present moment. For the most part, most of us are as dumb as a box of rocks and always miss the point. I had missed a very monumental point, so rocks are indeed smarter than me!

I blew the lamp out and sat, finishing the bottle and listening to my mentor settle into slumber. There wasn't any moonlight, but I could make out rough images of our abode. Finishing the last of the drink, I got up and went out into the night air; it would be a clear day tomorrow, and I'd get up early to head to the church to get some real coffee and pastries that they gave out once each week. With my waterworks done, I went back into the house and lay on my pallet and stared at the ceiling, counting the holes until I fell into a comfortable sleep.

I woke up the next morning facing the wall away from Shoes. I knew by sound that he had not yet risen. As I continued the exercise discerning any other presence, I was satisfied that there was no one here but us chickens, and moved into silent action not to disturb the old man. I quickly removed my shoes and got my feet in proper order; my plan was to head directly to the church for coffee and pastries. I knew it was early, so there was no need to rush. After my foot ministrations I glanced at Shoes, who was still sleeping soundly, shoes and bag where he left them beside him. I gathered my belongings and headed out, hoping to surprise him with a good cup of joe and dainties fit for a king. Stepping from the shed, I realized, indeed, this was going to be a good day.

I had talked with the pastor, who had said that there were things at the rectory that needed to be done and that we could handyman the winter behind the parsonage. There was a building that, in days gone by, had running water and indoor plumbing, an actual penthouse for tramps like us. I, knowing that Shoes was not fit to travel at length, thought this might be a way to doctor on him through the winter and have him better for spring travel. I had been thinking of a way to broach the subject and had figured it would come on its own accord.

Greeting locals and observing the shantytown, I noticed, like with other communities, how amazing it was, as always, that it came to life after sleep. Walking around to the fellowship hall, I met several nomads and exchanged the day's greetings. Coming through the door, I was greeted by the old couple in charge of this outreach and exchanged the pleasantries of the goodness of God. I got two large cups of hot coffee, making sure not to fill them completely to the brim, and placed the takeaway lids on them. I went to the pastry table and got four large bear claws drenched in glaze, wrapping them in paper towels to place in my jacket pockets, leaving my hands free to carry the steaming coffee. On my way out, the pastor was coming up the sidewalk. I stopped and spoke with him and told him that perhaps I'd talk to Shoes today about his proposal. I was concerned for him and felt that moving into a more accommodating place might help in his recovery. The pastor agreed and hoped he'd take him up on the offer. Promising to attend church services, which we always did, but never really having the commitment to do so was our standard in exiting conversations with the religious. Of course, that would have to change if we accepted to work for the church. It was always about respect. I smiled to myself as I thought on these things.

Continuing toward our shed, I thought of many things, each one about Shoes and me and what we should or should not do. With these thoughts dancing in my mind, I opened our door and placed his coffee and the pastries within arm's length of him, careful that he wouldn't have an accidental spill, then I sat on my mat and blew into my cup. Drinking the bliss of real coffee was a great feeling. I reached into my pocket to remove my bear claws, the glaze having mashed into the paper towel, and the aroma was heavenly as I peeled it from the morsel. So caught up in my own delight, I had no immediate thoughts of Shoes. I deemed it time to wake the master, but before I took his bear claws from my pocket, and of course they were in the same state as mine, squished. So I decided to make them more presentable. I got up and found a tin pan and placed them on it and then attempted to give them a rudiment of their previous form. After much finger-licking and repositioning, I felt they were ready for presentation. I set them beside the cooling coffee, which I wrapped on a cloth to help retain some heat.

On one knee, I placed my hand on his shoulder and gently shook him. "Shoes, got coffee and doughnuts. Man, you're going to sleep the day away!" I got a little closer, because his back was turned from me, and shook him a little firmer, repeating what I had just said. There was no movement. A quiet stillness. I rose from my knees and walked around the fetal-curled form under the blanket. I stood for a moment, and I still remember now the smell of that coffee and how it filled the small space of air. Slowly I got down on my knees and looked into what I could see of his hidden face in the blanket. I reached out my hand and moved the small part of the covering to be able to see all his face. He slept with just a hint of a smile; there were no deep crevices of lifelines. My friend was sleeping the eternal sleep. I don't know whether it was a natural thing to do or not, but I shook him once more. I called his name once more, but there was no answer. The answer came as I began to fit together all the pieces of hints that clearly showed through in the preceding days. The postal packaging, Whiskey going west, Shoes removing his shoes at night, and the bag—yes, the bag—always prepared for travel, especially getting it ready at night. I missed these puzzle pieces and truly what they represented. But I didn't beat myself about it, nor did I admonish myself for my ignorance. No, I looked at my friend just a while longer and replaced the cover to where it had been before. I rose to my feet and returned to my space.

I sat on the floor across from the still figure. All was quiet, and I heard the birds chirping and felt the breeze of mixture of cool and warmth waft easily into the abode. As I leaned my head against the wall, my mind no longer ticked out any commands of immediate necessity. No feelings tumbled within my breast. Nothing. Not even the sound of my own breath. Silence, deep, profound silence, permeated. I hummed the soul song, and I felt the boon of its presence. And then I drifted.

"Michael, have you ever heard the saying that a bird in hand is better than two in the bush?" said my martial arts master and mentor.

"Yes, sensei," I replied as I sat before the small space heater.

He continued as he watched me through sad old eyes, "That saying is both true and untrue. What must be considered, *always* considered, is what type of bird you have in hand. If what you hold in hand is death and destruction, perhaps there's a chance that those that are in the bush contain life and hope. Maybe you'll release what is in your hand and not capture none that is in the bush and be left with nothing, so to speak. One thing that will occur for certain: you will have released the known factor of your suffering and certain terrible end. We cannot avoid death, for death is an appointed end. This is a fact. To be born is to die. Much time is spent in life attempting to avoid this inevitability. Therefore, it is not to waste the value of living in despair of the fear of death. No, we must thrive in life so that death becomes another transition in change, which is constant.

"What you've been holding is the certainty of death, but also the denial of true living. To continue as you are will be to choose true suffering and agony in this life. Then you die, perish, cease to exist, at least here in this realm. I cannot speak of what is beyond. I, just as others, have chosen to believe in the God of all things. Faith is what we call it. You may use any metaphor that you wish, but in the end, it is all the same. One must come to believe in that which is greater than them. This is the true seed of hope, which grows into faith and blossoms into the discipline to seek harmony. You have no harmony. You must begin the journey or, indeed, you will die—not just die, but live in death each day until your body dies.

"Sometimes, a man must simply disappear. Perhaps you perish in the wandering. However, one way is a definite end. The other becomes an unknown, to be written by fate."

That was the last conversation I had with my master. By the time I would make it back to my homeland, he would have passed years before my return. Please note that that dialogue did save my worthless life, and for this I am grateful.

As I misted back into the present, my eyes drew through the memory of that cold morning, after the previous night of debauchery and mayhem, before I found my master's door in the unyielding gray light of that cold morning. Shoes lay as still as a statue of marble, just as he had succumbed to the great sleep on the cardboard bed. My legs, which had been outstretched, I now folded into the lotus position, and I erected my spine and, with folded hands upon my lap, began my deep, slow intakes of air. Closing my eyes, I neither sought solace nor deny it, breathing as I had been taught long ago.

Time passed, and as I surfaced, becoming conscious, I felt the wetness on my cheeks and saw the small pool of tears held within my upturned cupped palm. Again, I looked at the still figure and felt at peace. With a deep inhale and an explosive exhale, I slowly stood. My mind, strangely, was not a turbulence of thoughts; it was calm, decisive, and quiet.

I began my ascent into the next phase of my life by emptying my road bag and inventorying the contents and selection of needed items. Looking about our domicile, I began gathering the essentials for sustainability. I did not start repacking; I knew to place all things in order beside the object that would carry them, to evenly distribute the weight. It was this state that my mind and body were in when I heard in my head, "You got to promise me to do what I told you. The shoes and the sidesaddle, I won't be needing them, but you will!" I knew that was Shoes, and yet I fought to not touch items I felt to be sacred. I would not grave-rob; I would not desecrate the dead! I would ignore this pounding statement from the departed.

The sun was fully in the sky, and the day promised no rain, the air still holding some warmth from the Indian summer. With all the essentials packed, I went to my friend, mentor, and brother and stood before him, saying, "Thank you for all that you've done for me and the laughter you taught me to keep. I will not forget you, old man, and every time I hear the whistle of a train, you will be brought back to my memory. I couldn't have asked for a better friend, and even though I know this is part of the road of life, I can't help but feel this isn't right, but out of respect I will do what you said. I love you, old man, and wherever you may be, be at peace and rest. Perhaps we'll meet again. Hell, at least this one meeting had been a trip, huh?" I spied the shoes and the sidesaddle; they stood beside him, and strangely enough, it looked as though he had set them in that position for me to remember to take them. How he lay in his final resting, by God, it looked as though he'd prepared for the final trip and just tidied up in the evening so that in the morning moving about would be easy and natural. I tried to ignore what was before me, but there was no denying the truth, and I knew the truth, whether I accepted it or not. With a final sleeve wipe at the last of my tears, I bade farewell and turned, gathering my supplies. I went out the door and softly closed the tomb.

I walked from the tomb, from the shantytown, heading southbound, as I was taught, without looking back, for I might leave a portion of essential that might save my life later. I was determined not to turn, though I, through disciplined steps, struggled with each one. Heaven pressed on me and hell quaked beneath my feet, and a great compelling swelled within me!

Turn, O son of the road, and go back and retrieve thine heritage!

Though I felt some strength and was quite well, with each footfall south I made, it took immeasurable fortitude and might to continue. I stopped, and having no other recourse other than the solid fact that I had to return from whence I'd come, to do what was demanded of me—whether to be damned or to be elevated, it had come to my choice—I turned and headed back to the dreaded tomb. I had not realized that I had come so far, so far that the shantytown was not to be seen for a while. The sun was past its noonday zenith, and the temperature unseasonably warm, but onward I trekked. This was despite the sweltering heat and the weight of my load.

I turned the knob with reverence and respect for the dead. There Shoes still lay quietly upon the makeshift bed. I walked to the items, which still called out to me. I sat and started what I would consider a desecrating act of removing my shoes. I noticed that my shoes, though worn, still were quite serviceable and that someone could use them. I picked one of Shoes's curb cutters up and inspected it. His were of a finer quality, less worn and would prove to have a much longer road life than mine. I whispered a prayer that God, in all his mercy, forgive me for this act. Our feet proved to be a perfect match, and I proceeded with the exchange quickly, but with reverence of the dead. Placing my old brogans in place of my replacements, I stood and thanked him yet again. Stooping, I retrieved his pack and cross-bodied it to balance my additional weight, and left the place for the second time that day. However, in walking away this time, I felt no magnetic pull from behind. The gently cooling north wind pushed me, gently, forward, and the direction south became my beacon. I had determined that a good place to rest and combine our contents together would be at the turning point earlier where I could go no farther and had turned back. That made more sense to me.

After a while, because of my focus on walking, up ahead I began to scan the area in recognition of my first stopping point. I selected a place away from the road that was concealed with abundant overgrowth. It would equally serve as a place that I could bed for the night, in case the process would take longer than I thought, or if I just decided that it was enough travel for the day. I was taking in mind that I had already traveled close to eight miles with the doubling back.

Finding the suitable site was easy. I then unloaded my packs, removed my shoes, and drank from my water container. I started by emptying Shoes's packet first and spreading the items. Pretty much they were identical to mine, as in usable supplies. I systematically opened my pack and condensed our supplies together in single containers and inspected my pack in regards to perhaps using his instead. It was during inspection that I found that he had a makeshift, hidden false bottom and a plastic bag that contained over five hundred dollars in various denominations of bills. I sat back and smiled, not so much because the windfall was mine, but because of the ingenuity and the charity of my gone friend. I replaced the money and made the decision that his pack was better and more suitable for the next leg of the journey. I decided also that I would travel a little more for the day.

Once I had completed my foot-resting ritual and an exchange of socks, I took Shoes's brogans and inspected them again, at leisure. I had been feeling an oddity, but not discomfort, in the right shoe. I chalked it off to the stepping that had been done in them by the previous owner. I placed my hand inside the shoe and banged the heel upon the ground to dislodge any debris. And what tumbled out was a small piece of plastic containing a slip of white paper. I put my hand into the shoe and felt along the sole and the upper leather and discovered rolls of something that had conformed to that small spacing. Now, I was really intrigued, so I did the same with the left shoe and found the same thing. I unlaced each shoe to open the tops as wide as possible without damage and started to gently get at these strange stowaways. What I found in each shoe were two twenty-dollar bills, one on each side of the shoe, and a fifty at the toe, which totaled ninety dollars in each shoe! This totaled six hundred and eighty dollars that would have been on these shoes at any given time! I pulled the liquor out, unscrewed the cap, and poured a droplet or two on the ground, pronouncing, "Here's to those that are not here any longer. To you, Shoes, the king of hobos!" I drank a couple of deep swallows, enough to feel the warmth spread and the ease of mind.

I sat for a while, and then, coming to terms with the fact that it was time to move, I set my old bag upon a rock, for it to be found, and the items that I deemed I could do without beside it. For any who could use them. And then I harnessed my bag and headed on the dusty road. I began the soul song and listened to nothing but the memories of my past. I was willing to step into the uncertain future as a man and not a child.

One more thing: remember that note that fell first out of the shoe? This is what it said: "You will live."

ABOUT THE AUTHOR

Michael J. Scott lives at the old home front in the suburbs south of Pittsburgh, Pennsylvania. His most frequent visitor is a feral cat named Miriam, whom his sister named.

Michael is a former US Navy corpsman and received his BS degree from Florida Southern College in Lakeland, Florida. After he received his drug and alcohol diploma from Community College of Allegheny County, employment was obtained at a local nonprofit outreach center as an adult services coordinator. Certifications from Pennsylvania as a recovery specialist and lay speaker for the Methodist Church afford him the opportunity to share his story on over twenty-five years of active addiction and recovery solutions available.

Mr. Scott has continued to practice martial arts throughout all his adventures, which total fifty-seven years. The founding of the Tao Shen Mu Institute has become his life's dream come true. It is the hopes of Master Scott to transmute the teachings of body, mind, and spirit to individuals and corporations on the methodology of selecting empowered living first.

His enjoyments are reading, journaling, music, visual arts, and listening to the quiet. He still enjoys taking on projects in reconstruction to keep his trade skills in carpentry and cement work up to par.

With a certainty, this tome will be one of the many.

CPSIA information can be obtained
at www.ICGtesting.com
Printed in the USA
BVHW080017120921
616415BV00001B/53

9 781662 449130